FIX-IT and FORGET-IT
BUDGET MEALS

Fix-It and Forget-It®
BUDGET
MEALS

Quick, Easy & Inexpensive
Slow Cooker & Instant Pot Recipes

HOPE COMERFORD
PHOTOS BY BONNIE MATTHEWS

Good Books
New York, New York

Contents

Welcome to *Fix-It and Forget-It Budget Meals!*

This cookbook contains 127 of our best budget-friendly meals. We've tried to choose recipes with less expensive ingredients that don't compromise on flavor! Budget-friendly does not mean tasteless! Each recipe in this cookbook comes from a home cook, just like you, who has served it with love to their own family and friends. There is truly something for everyone in this book! We've got recipes like Chicken Parmigiana, Beef Stroganoff, Enchilada Stack-Up, Cheesy Stuffed Cabbage, Breakfast for Dinner Casserole, Southwest Chicken Soup, Tasty Meatball Stew, and so much more!

When shopping on a budget, shop smarter, not harder. Find cuts of meat that are on sale and freeze them for later, or substitute proteins in recipes to cook it up right away. Stock up on frozen vegetables or canned vegetables when you see a sale. Make dry beans in large batches and freeze them into bags portioned out like cans for later use in recipes. Get creative in the kitchen! Does the recipe call for peas, but you have only green beans? Use those! Only you will be the wiser! In the end, your family will appreciate the effort you made to put a hot, home-cooked meal on the table.

Choosing a Slow Cooker

Not all slow cookers are created equal . . . or work equally as well for everyone!

Those of us who use slow cookers frequently know we have our own preferences when it comes to which slow cooker we choose to use. For instance, I love my programmable slow cooker, but there are many programmable slow cookers I've tried that I've strongly disliked. Why? Because some go by increments of 15 or 30 minutes and some go by 4, 6, 8, or 10 hours. I dislike those restrictions, but I have family and friends who don't mind them at all! I am also pretty brand loyal when it comes to my manual slow cookers because I've had great success with those and have had unsuccessful moments with slow cookers of other brands. So, which slow cooker(s) is/are best for your household?

It really depends on how many people you're feeding and if you're gone for long periods of time. Here are my recommendations:

For 2–3 person household	3–5 quart slow cooker
For 4–5 person household	5–6 quart slow cooker
For 6+ person household	6½–7 quart slow cooker

Large slow cooker advantages/disadvantages:

Advantages:
* You can fit a loaf pan or a baking dish into a 6- or 7-quart, depending on the shape of your cooker. That allows you to make bread or cakes, or even smaller quantities of main dishes. (Take your favorite baking dish and loaf pan along when you shop for a cooker to make sure they'll fit inside.)
* You can feed large groups of people, or make larger quantities of food, allowing for leftovers, or meals, to freeze.

Disadvantages:
* They take up more storage room.
* They don't fit as neatly into a dishwasher.
* If your crock isn't ⅔–¾ full, you may burn your food.

Small slow cooker advantages/disadvantages:

Advantages:
* They're great for lots of appetizers, for serving hot drinks, for baking cakes straight in the crock, and for dorm rooms or apartments.
* Great option for making recipes of smaller quantities.

Disadvantages:
* Food in smaller quantities tends to cook more quickly than larger amounts. So keep an eye on it.
* Chances are, you won't have many leftovers. So, if you like to have leftovers, a smaller slow cooker may not be a good option for you.

My recommendation:

Have at least two slow cookers; one around 3 to 4 quarts and one 6 quarts or larger. A third would be a huge bonus (and a great advantage to your cooking repertoire!). The advantage of having at least a couple is you can make a larger variety of recipes. Also, you can make at least two or three dishes at once for a whole meal.

Manual vs. Programmable

If you are gone for only six to eight hours a day, a manual slow cooker might be just fine for you. If you are gone for more than eight hours during the day, I would highly recommend purchasing a programmable slow cooker that will switch to warm when the cook time you set is up. It will allow you to cook a wider variety of recipes.

The two I use most frequently are my 4-quart manual slow cooker and my 6½-quart programmable slow cooker. I like that I can make smaller portions in my 4-quart slow cooker on days I don't need or want leftovers, but I also love how my 6½-quart slow cooker can accommodate whole chickens, turkey breasts, hams, or big batches of soups. I use them both often.

Get to know your slow cooker . . .

Plan a little time to get acquainted with your slow cooker. Each slow cooker has its own personality—just like your oven (and your car). Plus, many new slow cookers cook hotter and faster than earlier models. I think that with all of the concern for food safety, the slow cooker manufacturers have amped up their settings so that "High," "Low," and "Warm" are all higher temperatures than in the older models. That means they cook hotter—and therefore, faster—than the first slow cookers. The beauty of these little machines is that they're supposed to cook low and slow. We count on that when we flip the switch in the morning before we leave the house for ten hours or so. So, because none of us knows what kind of temperament our slow cooker has until we try it out, nor how hot it cooks—don't assume anything. Save yourself a disappointment and make the first recipe in your new slow cooker on a day when you're at home. Cook it for the shortest amount of time the recipe calls for. Then, check the food to see if it's done. Or if you start smelling food that seems to be finished, turn off the cooker and rescue your food.

Also, all slow cookers seem to have a "hot spot," which is of great importance to know, especially when baking with your slow cooker. This spot may tend to burn food in that area if you're not careful. If you're baking directly in your slow cooker, I recommend covering the "hot spot" with some foil.

Take notes . . .

Don't be afraid to make notes in your cookbook. It's yours! Chances are, it will eventually get passed down to someone in your family and they will love and appreciate all of your musings. Take note of which slow cooker you used and exactly how long it took to cook the recipe. The next time you make it, you won't need to try to remember. Apply what you learned to the next recipes you make in your cooker. If another recipe says it needs to cook 7–9 hours, and you've discovered your slow cooker cooks on the faster side, cook that recipe for 6–6½ hours and then check it. You can always cook a recipe longer—but you can't reverse things if it's overdone.

Get creative . . .

If you know your morning is going to be hectic, prepare everything the night before, take it out so the crock warms up to room temperature when you first get up in the morning, then plug it in and turn it on as you're leaving the house.

   If you want to make something that has a short cook time and you're going to be gone longer than that, cook it the night before and refrigerate it for the next day. Warm it up when you get home. Or, cook those recipes on the weekend when you know you'll be home and eat them later in the week.

Slow Cooker Tips and Tricks and Other Things You May Not Know

- Slow cookers tend to work best when they're ⅔ to ¾ of the way full. You may need to increase the cooking time if you've exceeded that amount, or reduce it if you've put in less than that. If you're going to exceed that limit, it would be best to reduce the recipe, or split it between two slow cookers. (Remember how I suggested owning at least two or three slow cookers?)

- Keep your veggies on the bottom. That puts them in more direct contact with the heat. The fuller your slow cooker, the longer it will take its contents to cook. Also, the more densely packed the cooker's contents are, the longer they will take to cook. And finally, the larger the chunks of meat or vegetables, the more time they will need to cook.

- Keep the lid on! Every time you take a peek, you lose 20 minutes of cooking time. Please take this into consideration each time you lift the lid! I know, some of you can't help yourself and are going to lift anyway. Just don't forget to tack 20 minutes onto your cook time for each time you peeked!

- Sometimes it's beneficial to remove the lid. If you'd like your dish to thicken a bit, take the lid off during the last half hour to hour of cooking time.
- If you have a big slow cooker (7- to 8-quart), you can cook a small batch in it by putting the recipe ingredients into an oven-safe baking dish or baking pan and then placing that into the cooker's crock. First, put a trivet or some metal jar rings on the bottom of the crock, and then set your dish or pan on top of them. Or a loaf pan may "hook onto" the top ridges of the crock belonging to a large oval cooker and hang there straight and securely, "baking" a cake or quick bread. Cover the cooker and flip it on.
- The outside of your slow cooker will be hot! Please remember to keep it out of reach of children and keep that in mind for yourself as well!
- Get yourself a quick-read meat thermometer and use it! This helps remove the question of whether or not your meat is fully cooked, and helps prevent you from overcooking your meat as well.
  - Internal Cooking Temperatures: Beef—125–130°F (rare); 140–145°F (medium); 160°F (well-done)
  - Pork—140–145°F (rare); 145–150°F (medium); 160°F (well-done)
  - Turkey and Chicken—165°F
  - Frozen meat: The basic rule of thumb is, don't put frozen meat into the slow cooker. The meat does not reach the proper internal temperature in time. This especially applies to thick cuts of meat! Proceed with caution!
- Add fresh herbs 10 minutes before the end of the cooking time to maximize their flavor.
- If your recipe calls for cooked pasta, add it 10 minutes before the end of the cooking time if the cooker is on High; 30 minutes before the end of the cooking time if it's on Low. Then the pasta won't get mushy.
- If your recipe calls for sour cream or cream, stir it in 5 minutes before the end of the cooking time. You want it to heat but not boil or simmer.
- Approximate Slow Cooker Temperatures (Remember, each slow cooker is different):
  - High—212°F–300°F
  - Low—170°F–200°F
  - Simmer—185°F
  - Warm—165°F
- Cooked beans freeze well. Store them in freezer bags (squeeze the air out first) or freezer boxes. Cooked and dried bean measurements:
  - 16-oz. can, drained = about 1¾ cups beans
  - 19-oz. can, drained = about 2 cups beans
  - 1 lb. dried beans (about 2½ cups) = 5 cups cooked beans

What Is an Instant Pot?

In short, an Instant Pot is a digital pressure cooker that also has multiple other functions. Not only can it be used as a pressure cooker, but depending on which model Instant Pot you have, you can set it to do things like sauté, cook rice, grains, porridge, soup/stew, beans/chili, porridge, meat, poultry, cake, eggs, and make yogurt. You can use the Instant Pot to steam or slow cook or even set it manually. Because the Instant Pot has so many functions, it takes away the need for multiple appliances on your counter and allows you to use fewer pots and pans.

Getting Started with Your Instant Pot

Get to Know Your Instant Pot . . .

The very first thing most Instant Pot owners do is called the water test. It helps you get to know your Instant Pot a bit, familiarizes you with it, and might even take a bit of your apprehension away (because if you're anything like me, I was scared to death to use it).

Step 1: Plug in your Instant Pot. This may seem obvious to some, but when we're nervous about using a new appliance, sometimes we forget things like this.

Step 2: Make sure the inner pot is inserted in the cooker. You should *never* attempt to cook anything in your device without the inner pot, or you will ruin your Instant Pot. Food should never come into contact with the actual housing unit.

Step 3: The inner pot has lines for each cup. Fill the inner pot with water until it reaches the 3-cup line.

Step 4: Check the sealing ring to be sure it's secure and in place. You should not be able to move it around. If it's not in place properly, you may experience issues with the pot letting out a lot of steam while cooking, or not coming to pressure.

Step 5: Seal the lid. There is an arrow on the lid between and "open" and "close." There is also an arrow on the top of the base of the Instant Pot between a picture of a locked lock and an unlocked lock. Line those arrows up, then turn the lid toward the picture of the lock (left).You will hear a noise that will indicate the lid is locked. If you do not hear a noise, it's not locked. Try it again.

Step 6: *Always* check to see if the steam valve on top of the lid is turned to "sealing." If it's not on "sealing" and is on "venting," it will not be able to come to pressure.

Step 7: Press the "Steam" button and use the +/- arrow to set it to 2 minutes. Once it's at the desired time, you don't need to press anything else. In a few seconds, the Instant Pot will begin all on its own. For those of us with digital slow cookers, we have a tendency to look for the "start" button, but there isn't one on the Instant Pot.

Step 8: Now you wait for the "magic" to happen! The cooking will begin once the device comes to pressure. This can take anywhere from 5 to 30 minutes, in my experience. Then, you will see the countdown happen (from the time you set it for). After that, the Instant Pot will beep, which means your meal is done!

Step 9: Your Instant Pot will now automatically switch to "warm" and begin a count of how many minutes it's been on warm. The next part is where you either wait for the NPR, or natural pressure release (the pressure releases on its own), or do what's called a QR, or quick release (you manually release the pressure). Which method you choose depends on what you're cooking, but in this case, you can choose either, because it's just water. For NPR, you will wait for the lever to move all the way back over to "venting" and watch the pinion (float valve) next to the lever. It will be flush with the lid when at full pressure and will drop when the pressure is done releasing. If you choose QR, be very careful not to have your hands over the vent, as the steam is very hot and you can burn yourself.

The Three Most Important Buttons You Need to Know About

You will find the majority of recipes will use the following three buttons:

Manual/Pressure Cook: Some older models tend to say "Manual," and the newer models seem to say "Pressure Cook." They mean the same thing. From here, you use the +/- button to change the cook time. After several seconds, the Instant Pot will begin its process. The exact name of this button will vary on your model of Instant Pot.

Sauté: Many recipes will have you sauté vegetables, or brown meat before beginning the pressure cooking process. For this setting, you will not use the lid of the Instant Pot.

Keep Warm/Cancel: This may just be the most important button on the Instant Pot. When you forget to use the +/- buttons to change the time for a recipe, or you press a wrong button, you can hit "keep warm/cancel" and it will turn your Instant Pot off for you.

What Do All the Buttons Do?

With so many buttons, it's hard to remember what each one does or means. You can use this as a quick guide in a pinch.

Soup/Broth. This button cooks at high pressure for 30 minutes. It can be adjusted using the +/- buttons to cook more, for 40 minutes, or less, for 20 minutes.

Meat/Stew. This button cooks at high pressure for 35 minutes. It can be adjusted using the +/- buttons to cook more, for 45 minutes, or less, for 20 minutes.

Bean/Chili. This button cooks at high pressure for 30 minutes. It can be adjusted using the +/- buttons to cook more, for 40 minutes, or less, for 25 minutes.

Poultry. This button cooks at high pressure for 15 minutes. It can be adjusted using the +/- buttons to cook more, for 30 minutes, or less, for 5 minutes.

Rice. This button cooks at low pressure and is the only fully automatic program. It is for cooking white rice and will automatically adjust the cooking time depending on the amount of water and rice in the cooking pot.

Multigrain. This button cooks at high pressure for 40 minutes. It can be adjusted using the +/- buttons to cook more, for 45 minutes of warm water soaking time and 60 minutes pressure cooking time, or less, for 20 minutes.

Porridge. This button cooks at high pressure for 20 minutes. It can be adjusted using the +/- buttons to cook more, for 30 minutes, or less, for 15 minutes.

Steam. This button cooks at High pressure for 10 minutes. It can be adjusted using the +/- buttons to cook more, for 15 minutes, or less, for 3 minutes. Always use a rack or steamer basket with this function, because it heats at full power continuously while it's coming to pressure, and you do not want food in direct contact with the bottom of the pressure cooking pot or it will burn. Once it reaches pressure, the steam button regulates pressure by cycling on and off, similar to the other pressure buttons.

Less | Normal | More. Adjust between the *Less | Normal | More* settings by pressing the same cooking function button repeatedly until you get to the desired setting. (Older versions use the *Adjust* button.)

+/- Buttons. Adjust the cook time up [+] or down [-]. (On newer models, you can also press and hold [-] or [+] for 3 seconds to turn sound OFF or ON.)

Cake. This button cooks at high pressure for 30 minutes. It can be adjusted using the +/- buttons to cook more, for 40 minutes, or less, for 25 minutes.

Egg. This button cooks at high pressure for 5 minutes. It can be adjusted using the +/- buttons to cook more, for 6 minutes, or less, for 4 minutes.

Instant Pot Tips and Tricks and Other Things You May Not Know

- Never attempt to cook directly in the Instant Pot without the inner pot!
- Once you set the time, you can walk away. It will show the time you set it to, then will change to the word "on" while the pressure builds. Once the Instant Pot has come to pressure, you will once again see the time you set it for. It will count down from there.

- Always make sure the sealing ring is securely in place. If it shows signs of wear or tear, it needs to be replaced.
- Have a sealing ring for savory recipes and a separate sealing ring for sweet recipes. Many people report their desserts tasting like a roast (or another savory food) if they try to use the same sealing ring for all recipes.
- The stainless steel rack (trivet) the Instant Pot comes with can used to keep food from being completely submerged in liquid, like baked potatoes or ground beef. It can also be used to set another pot on, for pot-in-pot cooking.
- If you use warm or hot liquid instead of cold liquid, you may need to adjust the cooking time, or the food may not come out done.
- Always double-check to see that the valve on the lid is set to "sealing" and not "venting" when you first lock the lid. This will save you from the Instant Pot not coming to pressure.
- Use Natural Pressure Release for tougher cuts of meat, recipes with high starch (like rice or grains), and recipes with a high volume of liquid. This means you let the Instant Pot naturally release pressure. The little bobbin will fall once pressure is released completely.
- Use Quick Release for more delicate cuts of meat, such as seafood and chicken breasts, and for steaming vegetables. This means you manually turn the vent (being careful not to put your hand over the vent) to release the pressure. The little bobbin will fall once pressure is released completely.
- Make sure there is a clear pathway for the steam to release. The last thing you want is to ruin the bottom of your cupboards with all that steam.
- You *must* use liquid in the Instant Pot. The *minimum* amount of liquid you should have in the inner pot is ½ cup, but most recipes work best with at least 1 cup.
- Do *not* overfill the Instant Pot! It should only be ½ full for rice or beans (food that expands greatly when cooked) or ⅔ of the way full for almost everything else. Do not fill it to the max fill line.
- In this book, the Cook Time *does not* take into account the amount of time it will take the Instant Pot to come to pressure, or the amount of time it will take the Instant Pot to release pressure. Be aware of this when choosing a recipe to make.
- If the Instant Pot is not coming to pressure, it's usually because the sealing ring is not on properly, or the vent is not set to "sealing."
- The more liquid, or the colder the ingredients, the longer it will take for the Instant Pot to come to pressure.
- Always make sure that the Instant Pot is dry before inserting the inner pot, and make sure the inner pot is dry before inserting it into the Instant Pot.

- Use a binder clip to hold the inner pot tight against the outer pot when sautéing and stirring. This will keep the pot from "spinning" in the base.
- Doubling a recipe does not change the cook time, but instead it will take longer to come up to pressure.
- You do not always need to double the liquid when doubling a recipe. Depending on what you're making, more liquid may make the food too watery. Use your best judgment.
- When using the slow-cooker function, use the following chart:

Slow Cooker	Instant Pot
Warm	Less or Low
Low	Normal or Medium
High	More or High

Instant Pot Accessories

Most Instant Pots come with a stainless steel trivet. Below, you will find a list of common accessories that are frequently used in most Fix-It and Forget-It Instant Pot cookbooks. Most of these accessories can be purchased in-store or online.

- Steamer basket—stainless steel or silicone
- 7-inch nonstick or silicone springform or cake pan
- Sling or trivet with handles
- 1½-quart round baking dish
- Silicone egg molds

Breakfasts

Giant Pancake

Hope Comerford, Clinton Township, MI

Makes 4 servings
Prep. Time: 10 minutes   ☘   Cooking Time: 17 minutes

¾ cup whole wheat flour

¼ cup all-purpose flour

¾ tsp. baking powder

¾ tsp. baking soda

1 large egg

1¼ cups milk

1½ Tbsp. applesauce

Nonstick cooking spray

1 cup water

*Serving suggestion:
Serve with maple syrup, a
drizzle of honey, or topped
with your favorite fruit.*

1. In a bowl, mix the whole wheat flour, all-purpose flour, baking powder, and baking soda.

2. In a smaller bowl, mix the egg, milk, and applesauce until well combined. Pour into the dry ingredients and stir until well combined.

3. Spray a 7-inch round springform pan with nonstick cooking spray and then pour the pancake batter into it.

4. Pour the water into the inner pot of the Instant Pot. Place the springform pan on the trivet and carefully lower the trivet into the inner pot.

5. Secure the lid and make sure the vent is set to sealing.

6. Manually set your Instant Pot to Low pressure and set the cook time for 17 minutes.

7. When the cook time is over, manually release the pressure.

8. Remove the lid and carefully lift the trivet out with oven mitts.

9. Remove the cake from the pan and allow to cool for a few minutes before serving and to allow the moisture on the surface of the cake to dry.

Pumpkin Spice Pancake Bites

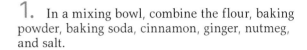

Hope Comerford, Clinton Township, MI

Makes 14 pancake bites
Prep. Time: 10 minutes ⚬ Cooking Time: 14 minutes

1 cup flour
1 tsp. baking powder
½ tsp. baking soda
½ tsp. cinnamon
¼ tsp. ground ginger
¼ tsp. nutmeg
Pinch salt
¾ cup pumpkin puree
1 cup milk
1 tsp. vanilla extract
1 large egg, beaten
Nonstick cooking spray
1½ cups water

1. In a mixing bowl, combine the flour, baking powder, baking soda, cinnamon, ginger, nutmeg, and salt.

2. Stir in the pumpkin, milk, vanilla, and egg until all ingredients are well mixed.

3. Spray 2 silicone egg bite molds with nonstick cooking spray. Place 2 Tbsp. of batter into each cup of the molds. Cover each filled egg bite mold tightly with foil.

4. Pour the water into the inner pot of the Instant Pot and set the trivet on top.

5. Stack the filled silicone egg molds onto one another on top of the trivet in the inner pot.

6. Secure the lid and set the vent to sealing.

7. With the Manual setting, set the cook time to 14 minutes on high pressure.

8. When the cooking time is over, let the pressure release naturally for 5 minutes, then manually release the rest of the pressure.

9. Carefully remove the trivet with oven mitts, uncover the egg bite molds, and pop out your pancake bites onto a plate or serving platter.

Serving suggestion:
Serve alongside some apple slices and with a bit of maple syrup for dipping the Pumpkin Spice Pancake Bites in.

Caramel Rolls

Jessalyn Wantland, Paris, TX

Makes 6–8 servings

Prep. Time: 20 minutes ⚘ *Cooking Time: 2–3 hours* ⚘ *Ideal slow-cooker size: 5 qt.*

½ cup brown sugar
½ tsp. ground cinnamon
4 Tbsp. (½ stick) butter
2 (8-oz.) pkgs. refrigerator biscuits

1. Mix sugar and cinnamon together in small bowl.

2. Melt butter in another small bowl.

3. Dip individual biscuits into melted butter and then into cinnamon and sugar mixture.

4. Place each covered biscuit in greased crock.

5. Cover and cook on High for 2–3 hours, or until rolls are done. Check rolls in center after 2 hours to see if they are done.

French-Toast Casserole

Michele Ruvola, Vestal, NY

Makes 9 servings
Prep. Time: 30 minutes ⚜ Cooking Time: 2–4 hours ⚜ Ideal slow-cooker size: 5–6½-qt.

2 eggs

2 egg whites

1½ cups milk, preferably 2%

5 Tbsp. honey, *divided*

1 tsp. vanilla extract

2 tsp. ground cinnamon, *divided*

3 cups finely diced apple

⅓ cup chopped, toasted pecans, *optional*

1 tsp. lemon juice

9 slices bread of your choice

1. In a mixing bowl, whisk together eggs, egg whites, milk, 2 Tbsp. honey, vanilla, and 1 tsp. cinnamon.

2. Separately, combine apples, remaining 3 Tbsp. honey, optional pecans, remaining 1 tsp. cinnamon, and lemon juice. Set aside.

3. In greased slow cooker, place one layer of bread, cutting to fit (triangles are good).

4. Layer in ¼ of the apple filling. Repeat layers, making 3 layers of bread and 4 of filling, ending with filling on top.

5. Pour egg mixture gently over all.

6. Cover and cook on High 2–2½ hours or Low 4 hours, or until bread has soaked up the liquid and apples are soft.

Variations:

You can use 3 diced bananas instead of apples. You may also use soy milk or almond milk instead of cow's milk.

Serving suggestion:

Serve with maple syrup.

Blueberry Fancy

Leticia A. Zehr, Lowville, NY

Makes 12 servings
Prep. Time: 10–15 minutes ⚹ *Cooking Time: 3–4 hours* ⚹ *Ideal slow-cooker size: 5-qt.*

1 loaf Italian bread, cubed, *divided*
1 pint blueberries, *divided*
8 oz. cream cheese, cubed, *divided*
6 eggs
1½ cups milk

1. Place half the bread cubes in the slow cooker.

2. Drop half the blueberries over top the bread.

3. Sprinkle half the cream cheese cubes over the blueberries.

4. Repeat all 3 layers.

5. In a mixing bowl, whisk together eggs and milk. Pour over all ingredients.

6. Cover and cook on Low until the dish is custardy and set.

Variation:
Add 1 tsp. vanilla to Step 5.

Serving suggestion:
Serve with maple syrup or blueberry sauce.

Poppy Seed Tea Bread

Julie Hurst, Leola, PA

Makes 10 servings

Prep. Time: 30 minutes ❧ Cooking Time: 3–4 hours
Standing Time: 30 minutes ❧ Ideal slow-cooker size: 6-qt.

½ cup whole wheat flour

1½ cups all-purpose flour

¾ cup sugar

2 tsp. baking powder

¼ tsp. salt

¼ cup poppy seeds

2 eggs, room temperature

8 Tbsp. (1 stick) salted butter, melted

¾ cup whole milk, room temperature

½ tsp. almond extract

½ tsp. vanilla extract

Serving suggestion:
Serve with pineapple whipped cream cheese and tea.

Tip:
If you don't have salted butter, add an additional ¼ tsp. of salt.

1. In a mixing bowl, combine flours, sugar, baking powder, salt, and poppy seeds.

2. Separately, whisk together eggs, butter, milk, and extracts.

3. Pour wet ingredients into flour mixture, stirring until just combined.

4. Make sure your loaf pan fits in your oval 6-quart slow cooker. Grease and flour loaf pan. Set it on a jar ring or other heat-resistant thing to keep it off the floor of the cooker.

5. Pour batter into prepared loaf pan.

6. Put lid on cooker, propping it open at one end with a chopstick or wooden spoon handle.

7. Cook on High for 3–4 hours, until tester inserted in middle comes out clean.

8. Wearing oven mitts (to protect your knuckles!), remove hot pan from hot cooker and allow it to cool for 10 minutes. Run a knife around the edge and turn loaf out on cooling rack to cool for an additional 20 minutes before slicing.

Breakfast Polenta

Margaret W. High, Lancaster, PA

Makes 8–10 servings

Prep. Time: 20 minutes ⚬ Cooking Time: 2½ hours ⚬ Ideal slow-cooker size: 5- or 6-qt.

4 eggs, room temperature

2 cups nonfat milk, room temperature

2 cups stone-ground (coarse) cornmeal

⅔ cup shredded Parmesan cheese, *divided*

4 cups boiling water

2 Tbsp. finely diced onion

2 cups chopped fresh spinach

1 tsp. kosher salt

Pepper to taste

1. In a large mixing bowl, beat eggs. Whisk in milk, cornmeal, and ⅓ cup Parmesan.

2. Whisk in boiling water.

3. Gently stir in onion, spinach, salt, and pepper.

4. Pour mixture into well-greased slow cooker.

5. Cover and cook on High for 2 hours, stirring once to be sure cornmeal is evenly distributed as it cooks.

6. When polenta is thick, sprinkle with remaining ⅓ cup Parmesan. Remove lid and allow to cook on High for an additional 30 minutes as cheese melts and any extra liquid evaporates. Polenta will be softer when hot, but will firm up as it cools. Serve hot, warm, or chilled.

Poached Eggs

Hope Comerford, Clinton Township, MI

Makes 2–4 servings
*Prep. Time: 5 minutes * *Cooking Time: 2–5 minutes*

1 cup water

4 large eggs

1. Place the trivet in the bottom of the inner pot of the Instant Pot and pour in the water.

2. You will need small silicone egg poacher cups that will fit in your Instant Pot to hold the eggs. Spray each silicone cup with nonstick cooking spray.

3. Crack each egg and pour it into the prepared cup.

4. Very carefully place the silicone cups into the Inner Pot so they do not spill.

5. Secure the lid by locking it into place and turn the vent to the sealing position.

6. Push the Steam button and adjust the time: 2 minutes for a very runny egg all the way to 5 minutes for a slightly runny egg.

7. When the timer beeps, release the pressure manually and remove the lid, being very careful not to let the condensation in the lid drip into your eggs.

8. Very carefully remove the silicone cups from the inner pot.

9. Carefully remove the poached eggs from each silicone cup and serve immediately.

Delicious Shirred Eggs

Hope Comerford, Clinton Township, MI

Makes 6 servings
Prep. Time: 5 minutes & Cooking Time: 2–3 minutes

Nonstick cooking spray

1 clove garlic, minced

2 Tbsp. fresh minced onion

6 Tbsp. milk, *divided*

6 jumbo eggs

6 Tbsp. grated fresh Parmesan cheese, *divided*

Fresh cracked pepper

1 cup water

1. Spray six ramekins with nonstick cooking spray.

2. Evenly divide the minced garlic and onion among the six ramekins.

3. Pour 1 Tbsp. of milk into each ramekin.

4. Break an egg into each ramekin.

5. Top each egg with 1 Tbsp. freshly grated cheese.

6. Season with fresh cracked pepper.

7. Pour the water into the inner pot of the Instant Pot. Place the trivet on top.

8. Arrange 3 ramekins on top of the trivet, then carefully stack the remaining 3 ramekins on top, staggering their positions so each ramekin on top is sitting between 2 on the bottom layer.

9. Secure the lid and set the vent to sealing.

10. Set the Instant Pot to low pressure and manually set the cook time to 2 minutes for runny yolks or 3 minutes for hard yolks.

11. When cook time is complete, manually release the pressure, and remove the lid. Serve immediately.

Egg Bites

Hope Comerford, Clinton Township, MI

Makes 14 mini quiches

Prep. Time: 15 minutes ⚬ Cooking Time: 11 minutes ⚬ Cooling Time: 5 minutes

2 tsp. olive oil

½ green bell pepper, diced

¼ cup finely chopped broccoli florets

½ small onion, diced

5 oz. fresh spinach

Nonstick cooking spray

8 eggs

¼ cup milk

3 drops hot sauce, *optional*

⅓ cup shredded cheddar cheese

1 cup water

1. In a small pan on the stove, heat the olive oil over medium-high heat. Sauté the bell pepper, broccoli, and onion for about 8 minutes. Add the spinach and continue to cook until wilted.

2. Spray 2 egg molds with nonstick cooking spray. Divide the cooked vegetables evenly between the egg bite mold cups.

3. In a bowl, whisk the eggs, milk, and hot sauce (if using). Divide this evenly between the egg bite mold cups, or until each cup is ⅔ of the way full.

4. Evenly divide the shredded cheese between the cups. Cover them tightly with foil.

5. Pour the water into the inner pot of the Instant Pot. Place the trivet on top, then place the 2 filled egg bite molds on top of the trivet, the top one stacked staggered on top of the one below.

6. Secure the lid and set the vent to sealing.

7. Manually set the cook time for 11 minutes on high pressure.

8. When the cook time is up, let the pressure release naturally for 5 minutes, then manually release the remaining pressure.

9. When the pin drops, remove the lid and carefully lift the trivet and molds out with oven mitts.

10. Place the molds on a wire rack and uncover. Let cool for about 5 minutes, then pop them out onto a plate or serving platter.

Serving suggestion:

Serve alongside your favorite healthy bread and a bowl of fruit.

INSTANT POT

Easy Quiche

Becky Bontrager Horst, Goshen, IN

Makes 6 servings, 1 slice per serving
Prep. Time: 15 minutes ⚹ Cooking Time: 25 minutes

1 cup water
Nonstick cooking spray
¼ cup chopped onion
¼ cup chopped mushrooms, *optional*
3 oz. shredded cheddar cheese
2 Tbsp. bacon bits, chopped ham, or browned sausage
4 eggs
¼ tsp. salt
1½ cups nonfat milk
½ cup whole wheat flour
1 Tbsp. soft margarine or butter

1. Pour the water into the inner pot of the Instant Pot and place the steaming rack inside.

2. Spray a 7-inch round baking pan with nonstick cooking spray.

3. Sprinkle the onion, mushrooms, shredded cheddar, and meat in the cake pan.

4. In a medium bowl, combine the remaining ingredients. Pour them over the meat and vegetables.

5. Place the baking pan onto the steaming rack, close the lid, and secure to the locking position. Be sure the vent is turned to sealing. Set for 25 minutes on Manual at high pressure.

6. Let the pressure release naturally.

7. Carefully remove the cake pan with the handles of the steaming rack and allow to stand for 10 minutes before cutting and serving.

Crustless Spinach Quiche

Barbara Hoover, Landisville, PA

Makes 8 servings
Prep. Time: 15 minutes ⚶ *Cooking Time: 2–4 hours* ⚶ *Ideal slow-cooker size: 3- or 4-qt.*

2 (10-oz.) pkgs. frozen chopped spinach, thawed completely

2 cups cottage cheese

¼ cup coconut oil, or any other oil you prefer

1½ cups cubed sharp cheddar cheese

3 eggs, beaten

¼ cup all-purpose flour

1 tsp. salt

1. Grease interior of slow-cooker crock.

2. Squeeze spinach as dry as you can. Then place in crock.

3. Stir in all other ingredients and combine well.

4. Cover. Cook on Low 2–4 hours, or until quiche is set. Stick blade of knife into center of quiche. If blade comes out clean, quiche is set. If it doesn't, cover and cook another 15 minutes or so.

5. When cooked, allow to stand 10–15 minutes so mixture can firm up. Then serve.

Kelly's Company Omelet

Kelly Bailey, Dillsburg, PA

Makes 12 servings

Prep. Time: 15 minutes   *Cooking Time: 7–9 hours*   *Ideal slow-cooker size: 6-qt.*

32-oz. bag frozen hash brown potatoes, or 5 cups cooked, shredded potatoes, *divided*

1 lb. ham, bacon, or sausage, cooked and chopped, *divided*

1 onion, chopped, *divided*

1 green bell pepper, chopped, *divided*

1 cup sliced fresh mushrooms, *divided*

2 cups shredded cheddar cheese, *divided*

12 eggs

1 cup whole milk

1 Tbsp. thyme, basil, rosemary, or tarragon, depending on what you like

½ tsp. cayenne pepper

1. In lightly greased slow cooker, place ⅓ of potatoes, ⅓ of ham, ⅓ of onion, ⅓ of green pepper, ⅓ of mushrooms, and ⅓ of cheese.

2. Repeat layers twice, ending with cheese.

3. In mixing bowl, whisk together eggs, milk, the herb you chose, and cayenne.

4. Pour gently over the layers in the slow cooker.

5. Cover and cook on Low 7–9 hours, until omelet is set in the middle and lightly browned at edges.

Western Omelet Casserole

Mary Louise Martin, Boyd, WI
Jan Mast, Lancaster, PA

Makes 10 servings
Prep. Time: 15 minutes   Cooking Time: 4–6 hours   Ideal slow-cooker size: 5-qt.

32-oz. bag frozen hash brown potatoes, *divided*

1 lb. cooked ham, cubed, *divided*

1 medium onion, diced, *divided*

1½ cups shredded cheddar cheese, *divided*

18 eggs

1½ cups milk

1 tsp. salt

1 tsp. pepper

1. Layer ⅓ each of frozen potatoes, ham, onion, and cheese in bottom of slow cooker. Repeat 2 times.

2. Beat together eggs, milk, salt, and pepper in a large mixing bowl. Pour over mixture in slow cooker.

3. Cover. Cook on Low 4–6 hours.

Serving suggestions:

Top with diced tomatoes or diced red peppers. Serve with orange juice and fresh fruit.

Shredded Potato Omelet

Mary H. Nolt, East Earl, PA

Makes 6 servings

Prep. Time: 15 minutes Cooking Time: 20 minutes

Nonstick cooking spray

3 slices bacon, cooked and crumbled

2 cups shredded cooked potatoes

¼ cup minced onion

¼ cup minced green bell pepper

4 eggs

¼ cup milk

¼ tsp. salt

⅛ tsp. black pepper

1 cup shredded cheddar cheese

1 cup water

1. With nonstick cooking spray, spray the inside of a round baking dish that will fit in your Instant Pot inner pot.

2. Sprinkle the bacon, potatoes, onion, and bell pepper around the bottom of the baking dish.

3. Mix together the eggs, milk, salt, and pepper in mixing bowl. Pour over potato mixture.

4. Top with cheese.

5. Add water to the inner pot, place the steaming rack into the bottom of the inner pot, and then place the round baking dish on top.

6. Close the lid and secure to the locking position. Be sure the vent is turned to sealing. Set for 20 minutes on Manual at high pressure.

7. Let the pressure release naturally.

8. Carefully remove the baking dish with the handles of the steaming rack and allow to stand for 10 minutes before cutting and serving.

Egg and Broccoli Casserole

Joette Droz, Kalona, IA

Makes 6 servings

Prep. Time: 15 minutes ⚶ *Cooking Time: 2½–3 hours* ⚶ *Ideal slow-cooker size: 4-qt.*

24-oz. carton small-curd cottage cheese

10-oz. pkg. frozen chopped broccoli, thawed and drained

2 cups (8 oz.) shredded cheddar cheese

6 eggs, beaten

⅓ cup flour

¼ cup melted butter, or margarine

3 Tbsp. finely chopped onion

½ tsp. salt

1. Combine all ingredients. Pour into greased slow cooker.

2. Cover and cook on High 1 hour. Stir. Reduce heat to Low. Cover and cook 2½–3 hours, or until temperature reaches 160°F and eggs are set.

Breakfast Casserole

Shirley Hinh, Wayland, IA

Makes 8–10 servings

Prep. Time: 15 minutes ❧ *Cooking Time: 3 hours* ❧ *Ideal slow-cooker size: 4-qt.*

6 eggs, beaten

1 lb. smoked cocktail wieners, or 1½ lb. bulk sausage, browned and drained

1½ cups milk

1 cup shredded cheddar cheese

8 slices bread, torn into pieces

1 tsp. salt

½ tsp. dry mustard

1 cup shredded mozzarella cheese

1. Mix together all ingredients except mozzarella cheese. Pour into greased slow cooker.

2. Sprinkle mozzarella cheese over top.

3. Cover and cook 2 hours on High, and then 1 hour on Low.

Breakfast Sausage Casserole

SLOW COOKER

Kendra Dreps, Liberty, PA

Makes 8 servings
Prep. Time: 15 minutes ⚬ Chilling Time: 8 hours
Cooking Time: 4 hours ⚬ Ideal slow-cooker size: 3-qt.

1 lb. meatless sausage crumbles
6 eggs
2 cups milk
8 slices bread, cubed
1 cup shredded cheddar cheese

1. In a nonstick skillet, brown and drain sausage.

2. Mix eggs and milk in a large bowl.

3. Stir in bread cubes, cheese, and sausage.

4. Place in greased slow cooker.

5. Refrigerate overnight.

6. Cook on Low for 4 hours.

Variation:

Use cubed cooked ham instead of sausage.

Breakfast for Dinner Casserole

Hope Comerford, Clinton Township, MI

Makes 4–6 servings

Prep. Time: 15 minutes   Cooking Time: 25 minutes

INSTANT POT

1 Tbsp. olive oil

½ lb. bulk breakfast sausage

½ cup finely diced onion

1 cup water

Nonstick cooking spray

½ lb. frozen Tater Tots or hash browns

6 eggs

¼ cup half-and-half

½ tsp. salt

½ tsp. garlic powder

¼ tsp. black pepper

⅛ tsp. cayenne pepper

½ cup diced bell pepper (any color you wish)

1 cup shredded pepper jack cheese

½ cup shredded cheddar cheese

Variation:

You can use any types of cheese that your family likes, or that you find on sale. Also, you could use bacon instead of sausage, or omit the meat altogether.

1. Set the Instant Pot to the Sauté function and add the olive oil.

2. Add the bulk sausage and onion to the inner pot of the Instant Pot and cook until browned. Remove it from the Instant Pot and set aside. Press the Cancel button.

3. Carefully wipe out the inside of the Instant Pot. Pour in the water and scrape the bottom, to be sure there is nothing stuck. Place the trivet on top with handles up.

4. Grease a 7-inch baking pan with butter or nonstick cooking spray. Arrange the Tater Tots or hash browns evenly around the bottom of the pan.

5. In a bowl, mix together the eggs, half-and-half, salt, garlic powder, black pepper, and cayenne. Stir in the bell pepper and pepper jack cheese. Pour this over the hash browns.

6. Sprinkle the cheddar over the top of the casserole. Cover with foil. Carefully lower the baking pan onto the trivet.

7. Secure the lid and set the vent to sealing. Manually set the cook time for 25 minutes on high pressure.

8. When the cook time is over, let the pressure release naturally for 10 minutes, then manually release the remaining pressure.

9. With hot pads, carefully remove the baking pan with the handles of the trivet. Uncover, serve, and enjoy!

Cheese Strata

Hope Comerford, Clinton Township, MI

Makes 6 servings
Prep. Time: 10 minutes ⚹ Cooking Time: 4–6 hours ⚹ Ideal slow-cooker size: 3-qt.

14 slices of bread, cut up or torn into bite-sized pieces

3 cups shredded sharp cheddar cheese

4 Tbsp. butter, cut into approximately 8 pieces

6 large eggs

3 cups milk, warmed for 3 minutes in the microwave

2 Tbsp. Worcestershire sauce

3–4 dashes hot sauce

1 tsp. garlic powder

1 tsp. onion powder

Salt and pepper to taste

1 small onion, chopped finely

1. Spray your crock well with nonstick spray.

2. Place half the bread in the bottom of the crock. Place 4 pieces of butter on top of the bread. Spread 1½ cups of the shredded cheese on top of that. Repeat this process with the remaining bread, butter and cheese.

3. Mix the eggs, milk, Worcestershire sauce, hot sauce, garlic powder, onion powder, salt, pepper, and onion together. Pour this mixture over the bread and cheese layers.

4. Cover and cook on Low for 4–6 hours.

Huevos Rancheros in the Crock

SLOW COOKER

Pat Bishop, Bedminster, PA

Makes 6 servings

Prep. Time: 25 minutes ⚘ *Cooking Time: 2 hours* ⚘ *Ideal slow-cooker size: 6-qt.*

3 cups salsa, room temperature

2 cups cooked beans, drained, room temperature

6 eggs, room temperature

Salt and pepper to taste

⅓ cup grated Mexican-blend cheese, *optional*

6 tortillas, for serving

Variation:

Serve with hot cooked rice instead of tortillas.

1. Mix salsa and beans in slow cooker.

2. Cook on High for 1 hour or until steaming.

3. With a spoon, make 6 evenly spaced dents in the salsa mixture; try not to expose the bottom of the crock. Break an egg into each dent.

4. Salt and pepper eggs. Sprinkle with cheese if you wish.

5. Cover and continue to cook on High until egg whites are set and yolks are as firm as you like them, approximately 20–40 minutes.

6. To serve, scoop out an egg with some beans and salsa. Serve with warm tortillas.

Serving suggestion:

Sprinkle with chopped cilantro or chopped spring onions before serving.

Insta-Oatmeal

Hope Comerford
Clinton Township, MI

Makes 2 servings
Prep. Time: 2 minutes   Cooking Time: 3 minutes

1 cup rolled oats
1 tsp. cinnamon
1½ Tbsp. maple syrup
Pinch salt
2 cups milk

1. Place all ingredients in the inner pot of the Instant Pot and give a quick stir.

2. Secure the lid and set the vent to sealing.

3. Press the Manual button and set the cooking time to 3 minutes.

4. When the cooking time is up, manually release the pressure.

5. Remove the lid and stir. If the oatmeal is still too runny for you, let it sit a few minutes uncovered and it will thicken up.

Serving suggestion:

Top with ¼ cup of your favorite fruits, like banana slices, raspberries, chopped strawberries, or blueberries.

Slow-Cooker Oatmeal

Martha Bender, New Paris, IN

Makes 7–8 servings

Prep. Time: 10–15 minutes ⚬ *Cooking Time: 8–9 hours* ⚬ *Ideal slow-cooker size: 4- to 5-qt.*

2 cups dry rolled oats

4 cups water

I large apple, peeled and chopped

I cup raisins

I tsp. cinnamon

1–2 Tbsp. orange zest

1. Combine all ingredients in your slow cooker.

2. Cover and cook on Low 8–9 hours.

3. Serve topped with brown sugar, if you wish, and milk.

Tip:

Zesting fruit is easy! If you don't have a fancy zesting tool, you can simply use a cheese grater.

Apple Oatmeal

Sheila Plock, Boalsburg, PA

Makes 6–8 servings

Prep. Time: 15 minutes ⚶ Cooking Time: 6 hours ⚶ Ideal slow-cooker size: 5-qt.

3–4 apples, peeled and sliced

½ cup brown sugar

1 tsp. nutmeg

1 tsp. cinnamon

2 Tbsp. (¼ stick) butter, cut in chunks

½ cup walnuts

3 cups uncooked rolled oats

6 cups milk

Variation:

You could substitute the apples with another fruit you prefer. Also, if you don't like walnuts, or they're not in the budget, leave them out, or sub them for another nut.

1. Layer apples in bottom of slow cooker.

2. Sprinkle with brown sugar, nutmeg, and cinnamon.

3. Dot with butter.

4. Scatter walnuts evenly over top.

5. Layer oats over fruit and nuts.

6. Pour milk over oats. Stir together until well blended.

7. Cover. Cook on Low 6 hours.

Baked Oatmeal

Ellen Ranck, Gap, PA

Makes 4–6 servings
Prep. Time: 10 minutes 🔹 Cooking Time: 2½–3 hours 🔹 Ideal slow-cooker size: 3-qt.

⅓ cup oil
½ cup sugar
1 large egg, beaten
2 cups dry quick oats
1½ tsp. baking powder
½ tsp. salt
¾ cup milk

1. Pour the oil into the slow cooker to grease bottom and sides.

2. Add remaining ingredients. Mix well.

3. Cook on Low 2½–3 hours.

Grain and Fruit Breakfast

Cynthia Haller, New Holland, PA

Makes 4–5 servings
Prep. Time: 5 minutes ⚶ Cooking Time: 3 hours ⚶ Setting: Slow Cook—Less or Low

⅓ cup uncooked quinoa

⅓ cup uncooked millet

⅓ cup uncooked brown rice

4 cups water

¼ tsp. salt

½ cup raisins or dried cranberries

¼ cup chopped nuts, *optional*

1 tsp. vanilla extract, *optional*

½ tsp. ground cinnamon, *optional*

1 Tbsp. maple syrup, *optional*

1. Wash the quinoa, millet, and brown rice and rinse well.

2. Place the grains, water, and salt in the inner pot of the Instant Pot. Secure the lid on top.

3. Cook on the Low or Less slow-cooker setting, or until most of the water has been absorbed, about 3 hours.

3. Add raisins and any optional ingredients and cook for 30 minutes more. If the mixture is too thick, add a little more water.

4. Serve hot or cold.

Slow-cooker option:

Use a 3-quart slow cooker. Follow directions above, but cook on Low for 3 hours in the slow cooker.

Serving suggestion:

Add a little milk to each bowl of cereal before serving.

Cynthia's Yogurt

Cynthia Hockman-Chupp, Canby, OR

Makes 16 servings
Prep. Time: 10 minutes ⚬ Cooking Time: 8 hours+ ⚬ Setting: Yogurt

I gallon 2% milk

¼ cup yogurt with active cultures

Note:

Spoon yogurt into containers and refrigerate. I store it in quart jars.

Serving suggestion:

When serving, top with fruit, granola, or nuts. If you'd like, add a dash of vanilla extract, peanut butter, or other flavoring. We also use this yogurt in smoothies!

1. Pour milk into the inner pot of the Instant Pot.

2. Lock lid, move vent to sealing, and press the yogurt button. Press Adjust till it reads "boil."

3. When boil cycle is complete (about 1 hour), check the temperature. It should be at 185°F. If it's not, use the sauté function to warm to 185°F.

4. After it reaches 185°F, unplug Instant Pot, remove inner pot, and cool. You can place on cooling rack and let it slowly cool. If in a hurry, submerge the base of the pot in cool water. Cool milk to 110°F.

5. When mixture reaches 110°F, stir in the ¼ cup of yogurt. Lock the lid in place and move vent to sealing.

6. Press Yogurt. Use the Adjust button until the screen says 8:00. This will now incubate for 8 hours.

7. After 8 hours (when the cycle is finished), chill yogurt, or go immediately to straining in step 8.

8. After chilling, or following the 8 hours, strain the yogurt using a nut milk bag. This will give it the consistency of Greek yogurt.

Granola in the Slow Cooker

Earnie Zimmerman, Mechanicsburg, PA

Makes 10–12 servings

Prep. Time: 10 minutes ⚬ *Cooking Time: 3–8 hours* ⚬ *Ideal slow-cooker size: 6-qt.*

5 cups rolled oats

1 Tbsp. flax seeds

¼ cup slivered almonds

¼ cup chopped pecans or walnuts

¼ cup unsweetened shredded coconut

¼ cup maple syrup or honey

¼ cup melted butter or oil of your choice

½ cup dried fruit

1. In slow cooker, mix together oats, flax seeds, almonds, pecans, and coconut.

2. Separately, combine maple syrup and butter. Pour over dry ingredients in cooker and toss well.

3. Place lid on slow cooker with a wooden spoon handle or chopstick venting one end of the lid.

4. Cook on High for 3–4 hours, stirring every 30 minutes, or cook on Low for 8 hours, stirring every hour. You may need to stir more often or cook for less time, depending on how hot your cooker cooks.

5. When granola smells good and toasty, pour it out onto a baking sheet to cool.

6. Add dried fruit to cooled granola and store in airtight container.

Variations:

Add whatever fruit or nuts you like. I've used dried cranberries, apples, and apricots. Pecans, walnuts, almonds, and sunflower seeds all taste delicious.

Serving suggestion:

Wonderful with milk or yogurt for breakfast.

Soups, Stews, Chilis & Chowders

Chicken Noodle Soup

Colleen Heatwole, Burton, MI

Makes 6–8 servings
Prep. Time: 15 minutes & Cooking Time: 4 minutes

2 Tbsp. butter

1 Tbsp. oil

1 medium onion, diced

2 large carrots, diced

3 ribs celery, diced

3 cloves garlic, minced

1 tsp. thyme

1 tsp. oregano

1 tsp. basil

8 cups chicken broth

2 cups cubed cooked chicken

8 oz. medium egg noodles

1 cup frozen peas (thaw while preparing soup)

Salt and pepper to taste

1. In the inner pot of the Instant Pot, melt the butter with oil on the Sauté function.

2. Add onion, carrots, and celery with large pinch of salt and continue cooking on sauté until soft, about 5 minutes, stirring frequently.

3. Add garlic, thyme, oregano, and basil and sauté an additional minute.

4. Add broth, cooked chicken, and noodles, stirring to combine all ingredients.

5. Put lid on the Instant Pot and set vent to sealing. Select Manual high pressure and add 4 minutes.

6. When time is up do a quick (manual) release of the pressure.

7. Add thawed peas, stir, adjust seasoning with salt and pepper, and serve.

Tips:

1. Rotisserie chickens are cheap and easy! I use them for all of my recipes that require cooked chicken because you can't beat the price, even by cooking a chicken yourself.

2. Bouillon cubes are a cheaper way of making broth and you do not have to boil the water ahead of time. For the recipe above, simply add 8 bouillon cubes and 8 cups of water to the crock. They will dissolve on their own while cooking.

Southwest Chicken Soup

Phyllis Good, Lancaster, PA

Makes 6–8 servings
Prep. Time: 15 minutes ⚬ *Cooking Time: 6½–10½ hours*
Chilling Time: 30 minutes ⚬ *Ideal slow-cooker size: 6-qt.*

3-lb. whole chicken, or chicken thighs

6 cups water

1 cup onion, chopped

1 cup celery, chopped

1½ Tbsp. olive oil

15½-oz. can black beans, rinsed

10-oz. pkg. frozen corn

15½-oz. can diced tomatoes

4-oz. can chopped green chilies

½ tsp. cumin

½ tsp. black pepper

2 tsp. chili powder

Salt to taste

½ cup cilantro, chopped

1. Place whole chicken in slow cooker. Add 6 cups water. Or place chicken thighs in cooker. Add 6 cups water.

2. Cover cooker. Cook on Low 5–8 hours, or until meat thermometer stuck into thickest part of the thigh (without touching the bone) registers 165°. Start checking at 5 hours, and do not overcook.

3. Remove whole chicken or thighs from cooker and allow to cool until you can handle the meat without burning yourself. Chop meat into bite-sized chunks. Set aside.

4. While chicken is cooking, sauté chopped onion and celery in olive oil in a skillet just until softened.

5. Add softened vegetables to broth in cooker, along with all remaining ingredients, except the cilantro.

6. Cover. Cook on Low for 2 hours, or on High for 1 hour, or until everything is heated through.

7. Ten minutes before serving, stir in chicken pieces. Heat.

8. Top individual servings with chopped fresh cilantro.

Chicken Rice Soup

Karen Ceneviva, Seymour, CT

Makes 8 servings

Prep. Time: 15 minutes ⚜ Cooking Time: 4½–8½ hours ⚜ Ideal slow-cooker size: 3½-qt.

½ cup wild rice, uncooked

½ cup long-grain rice, uncooked

1 tsp. vegetable oil

1 lb. boneless, skinless chicken thighs, cut into ¾-inch cubes

5¼ cups chicken broth

1 cup celery (about 2 ribs), chopped in ½-inch thick pieces

1 medium onion, chopped

2 tsp. dried thyme leaves

¼ tsp. red pepper flakes

1. Mix wild and white rice with oil in slow cooker.

2. Cover. Cook on High 15 minutes.

3. Add chicken, broth, vegetables, and seasonings.

4. Cover. Cook 4–5 hours on High or 7–8 hours on Low.

Serving suggestion:

A dollop of sour cream sprinkled with finely chopped scallions on top of each serving bowl makes a nice finishing touch.

Chicken Stew

Hope Comerford, Clinton Township, MI

Makes 6 servings
Prep. Time: 10 minutes   Cooking Time: 20 minutes

1 Tbsp. olive oil

1 cup chopped onion

3 carrots, chopped

2 celery stalks, chopped

4 cups chicken broth, *divided*

2 lb. boneless, skinless chicken thighs, diced

4–5 red potatoes, chopped

2½ tsp. salt

3 tsp. garlic powder

3 tsp. onion powder

1½ tsp. Italian seasoning

¼ tsp. pepper

2 bay leaves

2 Tbsp. cornstarch

2 Tbsp. cold water

1. Press Sauté on the Instant Pot. Let it get hot. Add the oil.

2. Sauté the onion, carrots, and celery for about 3–5 minutes.

3. Pour in 1 cup of the broth and scrape the bottom of the inner pot to bring up any stuck-on bits. Press Cancel.

4. Add the chicken, red potatoes, salt, garlic powder, onion powder, Italian seasoning, pepper, bay leaves, and remaining 3 cups of broth.

5. Secure the lid and set the vent to sealing. Manually set the cook time for 10 minutes on high pressure.

6. When cook time is up, let the pressure release naturally for 10 minutes, then manually release the remaining pressure. When the pin drops, remove the lid. Press Cancel.

7. Press the Sauté function once again. Mix the cornstarch and cold water, then stir it into the stew. Let it simmer for about 5 minutes, or until it is thickened. Remove the bay leaves before serving.

Tip:

Bouillon cubes are a cheaper way of making broth and you do not have to boil the water ahead of time. For the recipe above, simply add 4 bouillon cubes and 4 cups of water to the inner pot. They will dissolve on their own while cooking.

Serving suggestion:

My family loves stew with crusty Italian or French bread with butter on top.

Chicken Chili

Sharon Miller, Holmesville, OH

Makes 6 servings
Prep. Time: 15 minutes   Cooking Time: 5–6 hours   Ideal slow-cooker size: 4-qt.

2 lb. boneless, skinless chicken thighs, cubed

2 Tbsp. butter

2 (14-oz.) cans diced tomatoes, undrained

15-oz. can red kidney beans, rinsed and drained

1 cup diced onion

1 cup diced red bell pepper

1–2 Tbsp. chili powder, according to your taste preference

1 tsp. ground cumin

1 tsp. ground oregano

Salt and pepper to taste

1. In skillet on high heat, brown chicken cubes in butter until they have some browned edges. Place in greased slow cooker.

2. Pour one of the cans of tomatoes with its juice into skillet to get all the browned bits and butter. Scrape and pour into slow cooker.

3. Add rest of ingredients, including other can of tomatoes, to cooker.

4. Cook on Low for 5–6 hours.

Serving suggestion:

This is delicious when served topped with shredded cheddar cheese and sour cream.

White Chili

Esther Martin, Ephrata, PA

Makes 8 servings

Prep. Time: 15 minutes ⚜ *Cooking Time: 4–10 hours* ⚜ *Ideal slow-cooker size: 5-qt.*

3 (15-oz.) cans great northern beans, drained

8 oz. cooked and shredded chicken breasts

1 cup chopped onion

1½ cups chopped yellow, red, or green, bell peppers

2 jalapeño chili peppers, stemmed, seeded, and chopped, *optional*

2 cloves garlic, minced

2 tsp. ground cumin

½ tsp. salt

½ tsp. dried oregano

3½ cups chicken broth

Serving suggestion:

Ladle into bowls and top individual servings with sour cream, shredded cheddar cheese, and tortilla chips.

1. Combine all ingredients in slow cooker.

2. Cover. Cook on Low 8–10 hours, or on High 4–5 hours.

Tips:

1. You can often find frozen chopped peppers in the freezer section of your grocery store. This is often a less expensive option than fresh peppers.

2. Bouillon cubes are a cheaper way of making broth and you do not have to boil the water ahead of time. For the recipe above, simply add 3–4 bouillon cubes and 3½ cups of water to the crock. They will dissolve on their own while cooking.

Chili Chicken Corn Chowder

Jeanne Allen, Rye, CO

Makes 6–8 servings

Prep. Time: 15 minutes ☙ Cooking Time: 4 hours ☙ Ideal slow-cooker size: 4-qt.

1 large onion, diced

1 clove garlic, minced

1 rib celery, finely chopped

¼ cup oil

2 cups frozen, or canned, corn

2 cups cooked, deboned, diced chicken

4-oz. can diced green chilies

½ tsp. black pepper

2 cups chicken broth

Salt to taste

1 cup half-and-half

1. In saucepan, sauté onion, garlic, and celery in oil until limp.

2. Stir in corn, chicken, and chilies. Sauté for 2–3 minutes.

3. Combine all ingredients except half-and-half in slow cooker.

4. Cover. Heat on Low 4 hours.

5. Stir in half-and-half before serving. Do not boil, but be sure cream is heated through.

Tip:

Rotisserie chickens are cheap and easy! I use them for all of my recipes that require cooked chicken because you can't beat the price, even by making it yourself.

Navy Bean Soup

Joyce Bowman, Lady Lake, FL

Makes 8 servings
Prep. Time: 5 minutes ⚬ Soaking Time: 8 hours or overnight
Cooking Time: 8–10 hours ⚬ Ideal slow-cooker size: 5-qt.

1 lb. dry navy beans
8 cups water
1 onion, finely chopped
2 bay leaves
½ tsp. ground thyme
½ tsp. nutmeg
2 tsp. salt
½ tsp. lemon pepper
3 cloves garlic, minced
1 ham hock, or 1 lb. ham pieces

1. Soak beans in water overnight. Strain out stones, but reserve liquid.

2. Combine all ingredients in slow cooker.

3. Cover. Cook on Low 8–10 hours. Debone meat and cut into bite-sized pieces. Set ham aside.

4. Purée three-fourths of soup in blender in small batches. When finished blending, stir in meat.

Tip:

You can often find ham hocks in your local meat market. When I need just a little bit of ham, I buy ham steaks from my local grocery store.

Unstuffed Cabbage Soup

Colleen Heatwole, Burton, MI

Makes 4–6 servings
Prep. Time: 15 minutes   Cooking Time: 10–20 minutes

2 Tbsp. coconut oil

1 lb. ground beef, or turkey

1 medium onion, diced

2 cloves garlic, minced

1 small head cabbage, cored, chopped into roughly 2-inch pieces

6-oz. can tomato paste

32-oz. can diced tomatoes, with liquid

2 cups beef broth

1½ cups water

¾ cup white or brown rice

1–2 tsp. salt

½ tsp. black pepper

1 tsp. oregano

1 tsp. parsley

1. Melt coconut oil in the inner pot of the Instant Pot using Sauté function. Add ground meat. Stir frequently until meat loses color, about 2 minutes.

2. Add onion and garlic and continue to sauté for 2 more minutes, stirring frequently.

3. Add chopped cabbage.

4. On top of cabbage, layer tomato paste, tomatoes with liquid, beef broth, water, rice, and spices.

5. Secure the lid and set vent to sealing. Using Manual setting, select 10 minutes if using white rice, 20 minutes if using brown rice.

6. When time is up, let the pressure release naturally for 10 minutes, then do a quick release.

Tip:

Bouillon cubes are a cheaper way of making broth and you do not have to boil the water ahead of time. For the recipe above, simply add 2 bouillon cubes and 2 cups of water to the inner pot. They will dissolve on their own while cooking.

Nancy's Vegetable Beef Soup

Nancy Graves, Manhattan, KS

Makes 6–8 servings
Prep. Time: 10 minutes ⚬ *Cooking Time: 8 hours* ⚬ *Ideal slow-cooker size: 5- to 6-qt.*

2-lb. sirloin roast, cut into bite-sized pieces, or 2 lb. stewing meat

15-oz. can corn

15-oz. can green beans

1-lb. bag frozen peas

40-oz. can stewed tomatoes

5 beef bouillon cubes

Tabasco to taste

2 tsp. salt

1. Combine all ingredients in slow cooker. Do not drain vegetables.

2. Add water to fill slow cooker to within 3 inches of top.

3. Cover. Cook on Low 8 hours, or until meat is tender and vegetables are soft.

Variation:

Add 1 large onion, sliced, 2 cups sliced carrots, and ¾ cup pearl barley to mixture before cooking.

Chicken Tortilla Soup

Becky Fixel, Grosse Pointe Farms, MI

Makes 10–12 servings
Prep. Time: 5 minutes ⚘ *Cooking Time: 7–8 hours* ⚘ *Ideal slow-cooker size: 5-qt.*

2-lb. boneless skinless chicken breast

32 oz. gluten-free chicken stock

14 oz. verde sauce

10-oz. can diced tomatoes with lime juice

15-oz. can sweet corn, drained

1 Tbsp. minced garlic

1 small onion, diced

1 Tbsp. chili pepper

½ tsp. fresh ground pepper

½ tsp. salt

½ tsp. oregano

1 Tbsp. dried jalapeño slices

1. Add all ingredients to your slow cooker.

2. Cook on Low for 7–8 hours.

3. Approximately 30 minutes before the end, remove your chicken and shred it into small pieces.

Serving suggestion:

Top with a dollop of nonfat plain Greek yogurt, shredded cheese, fresh jalapeños, or fresh cilantro.

Instantly Good Beef Stew

Hope Comerford, Clinton Township, MI

Makes 6 servings
Prep. Time: 20 minutes ⚮ Cooking Time: 35 minutes

3 Tbsp. olive oil

2 lb. stewing beef, or beef sirloin, cubed

2 cloves garlic, minced

I large onion, chopped

3 celery stalks, sliced

3 large potatoes, cubed

2–3 carrots, sliced

8 oz. tomato sauce

10 oz. beef broth

2 tsp. Worcestershire sauce

¼ tsp. pepper

I bay leaf

Tip:

Bouillon cubes are a cheaper way of making broth and you do not have to boil the water ahead of time. For the recipe above, simply add 1 bouillon cube and 10 oz. of water to the inner pot. It will dissolve on its own while cooking.

1. Set the Instant Pot to the Sauté function, then add 1 Tbsp. of the oil. Add ⅓ of the beef cubes and brown and sear all sides. Repeat this process twice more with the remaining oil and beef cubes. Set the beef aside.

2. Place the garlic, onion, and celery into the pot and sauté for a few minutes. Press Cancel.

3. Add the beef back in as well as all of the remaining ingredients.

4. Secure the lid and make sure the vent is set to sealing. Choose Manual for 35 minutes.

5. When cook time is up, let the pressure release naturally for 15 minutes, then release any remaining pressure manually.

6. Remove the lid, remove the bay leaf, then serve.

Note:

If you want your stew to be a bit thicker, remove some of the potatoes, mash, then stir them back through the stew.

Pirate Stew

SLOW COOKER

Nancy Graves, Manhattan, KS

Makes 4–6 servings

Prep. Time: 15 minutes ❧ Cooking Time: 6 hours ❧ Ideal slow-cooker size: 4-qt.

¾ cup sliced onion

1 lb. ground beef

¼ cup uncooked, long-grain rice

3 cups diced raw potatoes

1 cup diced celery

2 (15-oz.) cans kidney beans, rinsed and drained

1 tsp. salt

⅛ tsp. pepper

¼ tsp. chili powder

¼ tsp. Worcestershire sauce

1 cup tomato sauce

½ cup water

1. Brown onions and ground beef in skillet. Drain.

2. Layer ingredients in slow cooker in order given.

3. Cover. Cook on Low 6 hours, or until potatoes and rice are cooked.

Meatball Stew

Barbara Hershey, Lititz, PA

Makes 8 servings
Prep. Time: 1 hour (includes preparing and baking meatballs)
Cooking Time: 4–5 hours ♣ Ideal slow-cooker size: 4- to 6-qt.

Meatballs:

2 lb. lean ground beef

2 eggs, beaten

2 Tbsp. dried onion

⅔ cup dried breadcrumbs

½ cup milk

I tsp. salt

¼ tsp. pepper

I tsp. Dijon mustard

2 tsp. Worcestershire sauce

Stew:

6 medium potatoes, unpeeled if you wish, and diced fine

I large onion, sliced

8 medium carrots, sliced

4 cups vegetable juice

I tsp. basil

I tsp. dried oregano

½ tsp. salt

½ tsp. pepper

1. In a bowl, thoroughly mix meatball ingredients together. Form into 1-inch balls.

2. Place meatballs on a lightly greased jelly-roll pan. Bake at 400°F for 20 minutes.

3. Meanwhile, to make stew, prepare potatoes, onion, and carrots. Place in slow cooker.

4. When finished baking, remove meatballs from pan. Blot dry with paper towels to remove excess fat.

5. Place meatballs on top of vegetables in slow cooker.

6. In a large bowl, combine vegetable juice and seasonings. Pour over meatballs and vegetables in slow cooker.

7. Cover cooker. Cook on High 4–5 hours, or until vegetables are tender.

Tips:

1. You can speed up the preparation of this dish by using frozen meatballs, either your own or store-bought ones.

2. You can make your own breadcrumbs, or even use finely crushed saltine crackers.

Easy Chili

Sheryl Shenk, Harrisonburg, VA

Makes 10–12 servings

Prep. Time: 15 minutes ⚬ Cooking Time: 3–8 hours ⚬ Ideal slow-cooker size: 6-qt.

I lb. ground beef

I onion, chopped

I green pepper, chopped

1½ tsp. salt

I Tbsp. chili powder

2 tsp. Worcestershire sauce

29-oz. can tomato sauce

3 (16-oz.) cans kidney beans, drained

14½-oz. can crushed, or stewed, tomatoes

6-oz. can tomato paste

1. Brown meat in skillet. Add onion and green pepper halfway through browning process. Drain. Pour into slow cooker.

2. Stir in remaining ingredients.

3. Cover. Cook on High 3 hours, or Low 7–8 hours.

Serving suggestion:

Serve in bowls topped with shredded cheddar cheese. This chili can also be served over cooked rice.

Tip:

You can often find frozen chopped peppers in the freezer section of your grocery store. This is often a less expensive option than fresh peppers.

Best Bean Chili

Carolyn Baer, Conrath, WI

Makes 6 servings

Prep. Time: 20–30 minutes ⚬ Cooking Time: 5–6 hours ⚬ Ideal slow-cooker size: 4- to 5-qt.

1 lb. ground beef

1½ cups chopped onion

1 cup chopped green bell pepper

1 tsp. minced garlic

1–3 Tbsp. chili powder, according to your taste preference

1–2 tsp. ground cumin, also according to your taste preference

15-oz. can red kidney beans, rinsed and drained

15-oz. can pinto beans, rinsed and drained

3 (14½-oz.) cans diced Italian-, or Mexican-, seasoned tomatoes

2 Tbsp. brown sugar

1 tsp. unsweetened cocoa powder

1–2 dashes soy sauce, *optional*

Sprinkle of ground ginger, *optional*

1. Spray large skillet with cooking spray. Brown beef in skillet over medium heat.

2. Add onion, bell pepper, and garlic to skillet. Cook until just-tender.

3. Transfer contents of skillet to slow cooker.

4. Add seasonings, beans, tomatoes, sugar and cocoa powder.

5. Cover. Cook on Low 5–6 hours.

Serving suggestion:

Offer a sprinkle of soy sauce and/or ground ginger with individual servings to enhance the flavor of the chili.

Tip:

You can often find frozen chopped peppers in the freezer section of your grocery store. This is often a less expensive option than fresh peppers.

Super Healthy Cabbage Soup

Hope Comerford, Clinton Township, MI

Makes 8–10 servings
Prep. Time: 10 minutes ✂ Cooking Time: 5 minutes

1 Tbsp. olive oil

1½ cups chopped onion

3 carrots, halved and sliced

2 celery stalks, halved and sliced

3–4 cups vegetable or chicken broth,
divided

14½-oz. can diced tomatoes

3 cups chopped cabbage

1 jalapeño, seeded and diced

1 Tbsp. garlic powder

3 tsp. salt

1 tsp. basil

1 tsp. oregano

¼ tsp. pepper

46 oz. tomato juice

1. Turn the Instant Pot to the Sauté function and let it get hot. Add the olive oil.

2. Sauté the onion, carrots, and celery for 3–5 minutes. Add 1 cup of the broth and scrape the bottom of the inner pot to get off any stuck-on bits. Press Cancel.

3. Add the remaining ingredients, including the remaining broth. You do not want to fill your pot all the way to the fill line. So, use a bit less broth if needed to not reach fill line.

4. Secure the lid and set the vent to sealing. Manually set the cook time for 5 minutes on high pressure.

5. When cook time is up, let the pressure release naturally for 10 minutes, then manually release the remaining pressure.

Tip:

Bouillon cubes are a cheaper way of making broth and you do not have to boil the water ahead of time. For the recipe above, simply add 3–4 bouillon cubes and 3–4 cups of water to the inner pot. They will dissolve on their own while cooking.

Mediterranean Lentil Soup

Marcia S. Myer, Manheim, PA

Makes 6 servings
Prep. Time: 10 minutes ⚭ Cooking Time: 18 minutes

2 Tbsp. olive oil

2 large onions, chopped

1 carrot, chopped

1 cup uncooked lentils

½ tsp. dried thyme

½ tsp. dried marjoram

3 cups chicken stock
or vegetable stock

14½-oz. can diced tomatoes

¼ cup chopped fresh parsley

¼ cup sherry, *optional*

⅔ cup shredded cheese, *optional*

1. Set the Instant Pot to the Sauté function, then heat up the olive oil.

2. Sauté the onions and carrot until the onions are translucent, about 5 minutes.

3. Press the Cancel button, then add the lentils, thyme, marjoram, chicken stock, and canned tomatoes.

4. Secure the lid and set the vent to sealing.

5. Manually set the cook time to 18 minutes at high pressure.

6. When the cooking time is over, manually release the pressure.

7. When the pin drops, stir in the parsley and sherry (if using).

8. When serving, add a sprinkle of shredded cheese if you wish.

Tips:

1. Bouillon cubes are a cheaper way of making broth and you do not have to boil the water ahead of time. For the recipe above, simply add 3 bouillon cubes and 3 cups of water to the inner pot. They will dissolve on their own while cooking.

2. You can use white vinegar, apple cider vinegar, or sherry vinegar instead of sherry.

Sweet Potato Lentil Soup

Joleen Albrecht, Gladstone, MI

Makes 6 servings
Prep. Time: 10–15 minutes ⚘ *Cooking Time: 6 hours* ⚘ *Ideal slow-cooker size: 4-qt.*

4 cups vegetable broth

3 cups (about 1¼ lb.) sweet potatoes, peeled and cubed

3 medium carrots, chopped

1 medium onion, chopped

4 cloves garlic, minced

1 cup dried lentils, rinsed

½ tsp. ground cumin

¼ tsp. salt

¼ tsp. cayenne pepper

¼ tsp. ground ginger

¼ cup fresh cilantro, minced, or 1–2 Tbsp. dried cilantro

1. Combine all ingredients in slow cooker.

2. Cover. Cook on Low 6 hours, or until vegetables are done to your liking.

Tip:

Bouillon cubes are a cheaper way of making broth and you do not have to boil the water ahead of time. For the recipe above, simply add 4 bouillon cubes and 4 cups of water to the crock. They will dissolve on their own while cooking.

Tuscan Bean Soup

Sara Harter Fredette, Williamsburg, MA

Makes 8–10 servings
Prep. Time: 10 minutes ⚶ Soaking Time: 1 hour
Cooking Time: 8–10 hours ⚶ Ideal slow-cooker size: 4-qt.

l lb. dry great northern, or other dry white, beans

8 cups water, *divided*

4 cups vegetable broth

2 cloves garlic, minced

4 Tbsp. chopped parsley

Olive oil

2 tsp. salt

½ tsp. pepper

1. Place beans in large soup pot. Cover with 4 cups water and bring to boil. Cook 2 minutes. Remove from heat. Cover pot and allow to stand for 1 hour. Drain, discarding water.

2. Combine beans, 4 cups fresh water, and broth in slow cooker.

3. Sauté garlic and parsley in olive oil in skillet. Stir into slow cooker. Add salt and pepper.

4. Cover. Cook on Low 8–10 hours, or until beans are tender.

Tips:

1. If you do not want to boil the beans, you can simply soak them overnight in water for 10–12 hours. In the morning, drain and rinse them.

2. Bouillon cubes are a cheaper way of making broth and you do not have to boil the water ahead of time. For the recipe above, simply add 4 bouillon cubes and 4 cups of water to the crock. They will dissolve on their own while cooking.

Black Bean Soup

Colleen Heatwole, Burton, MI

Makes 4–6 servings
Prep. Time: 10 minutes ⚬ Cooking Time: 40 minutes

2 cups dry black beans, cleaned of debris and rinsed

1 cup coarsely chopped onion

3 cloves garlic, minced

½ tsp. paprika

⅛ tsp. red pepper flakes

2 large bay leaves

1 tsp. cumin

2 tsp. oregano

½ tsp. salt (more if desired)

6 cups vegetable or chicken broth

Yogurt or sour cream, for garnish, *optional*

1. Place all ingredients, except the yogurt or sour cream, into the inner pot of the Instant Pot.

2. Secure the lid and set the vent to sealing. Manually set the cook time for 40 minutes on high pressure.

3. When cook time is up, let pressure release naturally for 10 minutes, then manually release the remaining pressure.

4. Open the lid. Remove the bay leaves and discard them. Serve with desired garnishes.

Tip:

Bouillon cubes are a cheaper way of making broth and you do not have to boil the water ahead of time. For the recipe above, simply add 6 bouillon cubes and 6 cups of water to the inner pot. They will dissolve on their own while cooking.

INSTANT POT

Cannellini Bean & Spinach Soup

Hope Comerford, Clinton Township, MI

Makes 6–8 servings
Prep. Time: 10 minutes ⚬ Soaking Time: overnight ⚬ Cooking Time: 30 minutes

2 Tbsp. extra-virgin olive oil

4 cloves garlic, sliced very thin

1 small onion, chopped

8 cups spinach

8-oz. bag dry cannellini beans, soaked overnight, drained and rinsed

8 cups chicken stock

3 basil leaves, chopped fine

Parmesan cheese shavings, *optional*

1. Set the Instant Pot to Sauté and heat the olive oil.

2. Sauté the garlic, onion, and spinach until the onion is translucent.

3. Hit the Cancel button on your Instant Pot and add the beans and chicken stock.

4. Secure the lid and set the vent to sealing.

5. Manually set the time for 25 minutes on high pressure.

6. When the cooking time is over, let the pressure release naturally. Remove the lid when the pin drops and spoon into serving bowls.

7. Top each bowl with a sprinkle of the chopped basil leaves and a few Parmesan shavings (if using).

Tips:

1. If you do not remember to soak the beans overnight, or if you don't have time to soak them, simply cook the soup on high pressure for 51 minutes instead.

2. Bouillon cubes are a cheaper way of making broth and you do not have to boil the water ahead of time. For the recipe above, simply add 8 bouillon cubes and 8 cups of water to the inner pot. They will dissolve on their own while cooking.

Grace's Minestrone Soup

Grace Ketcham, Marietta, GA

Makes 8 servings
Prep. Time: 15 minutes ⚬ Cooking Time: 8 hours ⚬ Ideal slow-cooker size: 4- to 5-qt.

¾ cup dry elbow macaroni

2 qt. vegetable broth

2 large onions, diced

2 carrots, sliced

½ head of cabbage, shredded

½ cup celery, *diced*

16 oz. can diced tomatoes

½ tsp. salt

½ tsp. dried oregano

I Tbsp. minced parsley

¼ cup each frozen corn, peas, and lima beans

¼ tsp. pepper

1. Cook macaroni according to package directions. Set aside.

2. Combine all ingredients except macaroni in large slow cooker.

3. Cover. Cook on Low 8 hours. Add macaroni during last 30 minutes of cooking time.

Serving suggestion:

Garnish individual servings with grated Parmesan or Romano cheese.

Tip:

Bouillon cubes are a cheaper way of making broth and you do not have to boil the water ahead of time. For the recipe above, simply add 8 bouillon cubes and 8 cups of water to the crock. They will dissolve on their own while cooking.

Veggie Minestrone

Dorothy VanDeest, Memphis, TN

Makes 8 servings
Prep. Time: 5 minutes ❧ Cooking Time: 4 minutes

2 Tbsp. olive oil

1 large onion, chopped

1 clove garlic, minced

4 cups chicken or vegetable stock

16-oz. can kidney beans, rinsed and drained

14½-oz. can diced tomatoes

2 medium carrots, sliced thin

¼ tsp. dried oregano

¼ tsp. pepper

½ cup whole wheat elbow macaroni, uncooked

4 oz. fresh spinach

½ cup grated Parmesan cheese

Tip:

Bouillon cubes are a cheaper way of making broth and you do not have to boil the water ahead of time. For the recipe above, simply add 4 bouillon cubes and 4 cups of water to the inner pot. They will dissolve on their own while cooking.

1. Set the Instant Pot to the Sauté function and heat the olive oil.

2. When the olive oil is heated, add the onion and garlic to the inner pot and sauté for 5 minutes.

3. Press Cancel and add the stock, kidney beans, tomatoes, carrots, oregano, and pepper. Gently pour in the macaroni, but do not stir. Just push the noodles gently under the liquid.

4. Secure the lid and set the vent to sealing.

5. Manually set the cook time for 4 minutes on high pressure.

6. When the cooking time is over, manually release the pressure and remove the lid when the pin drops.

7. Stir in the spinach and let wilt a few minutes.

8. Sprinkle 1 Tbsp. grated Parmesan on each individual bowl of this soup. Enjoy!

Veggie Stew

Ernestine Schrepfer, Trenton, MO

Makes 10–15 servings

Prep. Time: 15 minutes   Cooking Time: 9–11 hours   Ideal slow-cooker size: 8-qt.

5–6 potatoes, cubed

3 carrots, cubed

1 onion, chopped

½ cup chopped celery

2 cups canned diced,
or stewed, tomatoes

3 vegetable bouillon cubes

3 cups water

1½ tsp. dried thyme

½ tsp. dried parsley

½ cup brown rice, uncooked

1 lb. frozen green beans

1 lb. frozen corn

15-oz. can butter beans

46-oz. can V8® juice

1. Combine potatoes, carrots, onion, celery, tomatoes, bouillon cubes, water, thyme, parsley, and rice in 8-quart cooker, or two medium-sized cookers.

2. Cover. Cook on High 2 hours. Purée one cup of mixture and add back to slow cooker to thicken the soup.

3. Stir in beans, corn, butter beans, and juice.

4. Cover. Cook on High 1 more hour, then reduce to Low and cook 6–8 more hours.

Three-Cheese Broccoli Soup

Deb Kepiro, Strasburg, PA

Makes 8 servings

Prep. Time: 15 minutes ⚬ Cooking Time: 7–9 hours on Low or 4–6 hours on High

⚬ Ideal slow-cooker size: 4–5-qt.

4 cups chicken or vegetable broth

2 cups milk

2 (10-oz.) bags frozen broccoli florets

½ cup very finely diced white onion

½ tsp. black pepper

½ tsp. kosher salt

½ tsp. ground nutmeg

3 cups three different grated cheeses

Serving suggestion:
Serve with your favorite rolls or drop biscuits.

1. In slow cooker, combine broth, milk, broccoli, onion, pepper, salt, and nutmeg.

2. Cook on Low for 5–6 hours or High for 2–3 hours, until onion is soft.

3. Add cheese 20 minutes before serving. Cheese may be stringy and stick to broccoli—that's fine.

Tip:

Bouillon cubes are a cheaper way of making broth and you do not have to boil the water ahead of time. For the recipe above, simply add 4 bouillon cubes and 4 cups of water to the crock. They will dissolve on their own while cooking.

Potato Soup

Michele Ruvola, Vestal, NY

Makes 4 servings
Prep. Time: 20 minutes ⚬ *Cooking Time: 5 minutes*

5 lb. russet potatoes, peeled and cubed

3 celery stalks, sliced thin

I large onion, diced

I clove garlic, minced

I Tbsp. seasoning salt

I tsp. ground black pepper

4 Tbsp. (½ stick) butter

I lb. bacon, fried crisp, rough chopped

4 cups chicken stock or broth

I cup heavy cream

½ cup whole milk

Sour cream, shredded cheddar cheese, sliced green onions for garnish, *optional*

Tip:

Bouillon cubes are a cheaper way of making broth and you do not have to boil the water ahead of time. For the recipe above, simply add 4 bouillon cubes and 4 cups of water to the inner pot. They will dissolve on their own while cooking.

1. Put potatoes, celery, onion, garlic, seasoning salt, pepper, and butter in the inner pot of the Instant Pot. Stir to combine.

2. Add bacon and chicken stock, then stir to combine.

3. Secure the lid and make sure the vent is on sealing. Push the Manual mode button, then set timer for 5 minutes on high pressure.

4. Quick release the steam when cook time is up.

5. Remove lid; mash potatoes to make a semismooth soup.

6. Add cream and milk; stir to combine.

7. Serve with garnishes if desired.

Serving suggestion:

Perfect on a cold night with slices of bread on the side or a salad.

Potato and Corn Chowder

Janie Steele, Moore, OK

Makes 4–6 servings
Prep. Time: 10 minutes ⚹ Cooking Time: 10 minutes

3 Tbsp. butter

¼ cup diced onion

6 medium red potatoes, diced

4 ears corn, or frozen or canned equal to 2 cups

3 cups vegetable broth or water

2 tsp. cornstarch

3 cups half-and-half

Grated cheddar cheese, *optional*

Tip:
Bouillon cubes are a cheaper way of making broth and you do not have to boil the water ahead of time. For the recipe above, simply add 3 bouillon cubes and 3 cups of water to the inner pot. They will dissolve on their own while cooking.

1. Place the butter in the inner pot of the Instant Pot. Press the Sauté function and let the butter melt.

2. Sauté the onion in the butter until translucent.

3. Add the potatoes, corn, and 3 cups broth or water to the Inner Pot.

4. Secure the lid and set vent to sealing, then cook on Manual, high pressure, for 10 minutes.

5. Let the pressure release naturally, then remove lid.

6. Mix cornstarch in small amount of water and mix into soup to thicken.

7. With Instant Pot on sauté, add the half-and-half slowly while stirring.

8. Serve with cheddar cheese on top, if desired.

Main Dishes

Chicken & Turkey

Garlic Galore Rotisserie Chicken

Hope Comerford, Clinton Township, MI

Makes 4 servings
Prep. Time: 5 minutes ⚬ Cooking Time: 33 minutes

3-lb. whole chicken, innards removed

2 Tbsp. olive oil, *divided*

Salt and pepper to taste

20–30 cloves fresh garlic, peeled and left whole

1 cup vegetable broth

2 Tbsp. garlic powder

2 tsp. onion powder

½ tsp. basil

½ tsp. cumin

½ tsp. chili powder

1. Rub chicken with one tablespoon of the olive oil and sprinkle with salt and pepper.

2. Place the garlic cloves inside the chicken. Use butcher's twine to secure the legs.

3. Press the sauté button on the Instant Pot, then add the rest of the olive oil to the inner pot.

4. When the pot is hot, place the chicken inside. You are just trying to sear it, so leave it for about 4 minutes on each side.

5. Remove the chicken and set aside. Place the trivet at the bottom of the inner pot and pour in the vegetable broth.

6. Mix the remaining seasonings and rub the mixture all over the entire chicken.

7. Place the chicken back inside the inner pot, breast-side up, on top of the trivet and secure the lid to the sealing position.

8. Press the Manual button and use the +/- to set it for 25 minutes.

9. When the timer beeps, allow the pressure to release naturally for 15 minutes. If the lid will not open at this point, quick release the remaining pressure and remove the chicken.

10. Let the chicken rest for 5 to 10 minutes before serving.

Tip:

Bouillon cubes are a cheaper way of making broth and you do not have to boil the water ahead of time. For the recipe above, simply add 1 bouillon cube and 1 cup of water to the inner pot. It will dissolve on its own while cooking.

Serving suggestion:

This would be great alongside Potluck Baked Corn on page 189, or Broccoli with Garlic on page 192.

Tasty Drumsticks

Trudy Kutter, Corfu, NY

Makes 5–6 servings
Prep. Time: 20 minutes ⁂ Cooking Time: 6 hours ⁂ Ideal slow-cooker size: 5-qt.

3–4 lb. chicken drumsticks, skin removed
8-oz. can tomato sauce
¼ cup soy sauce
¼ cup brown sugar
1 tsp. minced garlic
3 Tbsp. cornstarch
¼ cup cold water

1. Place drumsticks in slow cooker.

2. Combine tomato sauce, soy sauce, brown sugar, and garlic in a bowl.

3. Pour over drumsticks, making sure that each drumstick is sauced.

4. Cover. Cook on Low 6 hours, or until chicken is tender.

5. Remove chicken with tongs to a platter and keep it warm.

6. Strain juices into saucepan.

7. In a bowl combine cornstarch and water until smooth.

8. Add cornstarch mixture to saucepan.

9. Bring mixture to a boil, stirring continuously.

10. Stir for two minutes until thickened.

Serving suggestions:
Serve sauce alongside, or spooned over, chicken.
   This would be great served over Perfect White Rice on page 178 and alongside Vegetable Medley on page 187.

Italian Chicken and Broccoli

Liz Clapper, Lancaster, PA

Makes 6 servings
Prep. Time: 15 minutes ⚹ Cooking Time: 5 minutes

1 tsp. olive oil

1 head broccoli, chopped into florets (about 4 cups)

2 cloves garlic, finely chopped

1 lb. boneless skinless chicken thighs, cut into strips

4 medium carrots, sliced thin

2 cups uncooked macaroni pasta

3 cups chicken broth

1½ Tbsp. Italian seasoning

¼ cup shredded Parmesan cheese

Serving suggestion:

This would be great served alongside Wild Rice on page 179 or Slow-Cooker Scalloped Potatoes on page 184.

1. Set the Instant Pot to Sauté and heat the oil.

2. Sauté the broccoli for 5 minutes in the inner pot. Set it aside in a bowl and cover to keep warm.

3. Add the garlic and chicken and sauté for 8 minutes.

4. Press Cancel. Add the carrots and stir. Pour the macaroni evenly over the top. Pour in the broth and Italian seasoning. Do not stir.

5. Secure the lid and set the vent to sealing.

6. Manually set the cook time for 5 minutes on high pressure.

7. When the cooking time is over, let the pressure release naturally for 5 minutes, then manually release the remaining pressure.

8. When the pin drops, remove the lid, sprinkle the contents with Parmesan, and serve immediately.

Tips:

1. For this recipe, you can use 12 oz. frozen broccoli florets in lieu of the fresh broccoli.

2. Bouillon cubes are a cheaper way of making broth and you do not have to boil the water ahead of time. For the recipe above, simply add 3 bouillon cubes and 3 cups of water to the inner pot. They will dissolve on their own while cooking.

Butter Chicken

Jessica Stoner, Arlington, OH

Makes 4 servings
Prep. Time: 10–15 minutes ⚬ *Cooking Time: 20 minutes*

1 Tbsp. olive oil

1 medium onion, diced

1–2 medium cloves garlic, minced

½ Tbsp. minced ginger

1 tsp. garam masala

½ tsp. turmeric

2 tsp. kosher salt

2 lb. cubed boneless, skinless chicken thighs

¼ cup tomato paste

2 cups crushed tomatoes

1½ cups water

½ Tbsp. honey

1½ cups heavy cream

1 Tbsp. butter

1. On Sauté function at high heat, heat the oil in the inner pot of the Instant Pot. Add the onion, garlic, and ginger and sauté for 1 minute, until fragrant and onion is soft.

2. Add the garam masala, turmeric, and salt. Sauté quickly and add the chicken. Stir to coat chicken. Add the tomato paste and crushed tomatoes. Slowly add the water, scraping the bottom of the pot with a spoon to make sure there are no bits of tomato stuck to the bottom. Stir in the honey.

3. Secure the lid, making sure vent is turned to sealing function. Use the Poultry high pressure function and set cook time to 15 minutes. Once done cooking, do a quick release of the pressure.

4. Remove lid and change to medium/normal Sauté function and stir in the heavy cream and bring to a simmer. Simmer for 5 minutes, adding up to ¼ cup additional water if you need to thin the sauce out. Stir in the butter until melted and turn off.

Serving suggestion:
Serve hot with basmati rice and naan, or over Perfect White Rice on page 178.

INSTANT POT

Chicken Stir-Fry

Hope Comerford, Clinton Township, MI

Makes 4–6 servings
Prep. Time: 5 minutes ⚬ Cooking Time: 16 minutes

2 lb. boneless, skinless chicken thighs

1 small onion, sliced

½ cup soy sauce or liquid aminos

¼ cup chicken stock or broth

1 clove garlic, minced

1 tsp. ginger

⅛ tsp. pepper

¼ cup cornstarch

¼ cup cold water

20-oz. bag frozen stir-fry vegetables

3 cups cooked rice

1. Place the chicken into the inner pot of the Instant Pot, along with the onion, soy sauce, chicken stock, garlic, ginger, and pepper.

2. Secure the lid and set the vent to sealing. Manually set the cook time for 7 minutes on high pressure. (This would be a good time to start the rice on the stove, or in a second Instant Pot. See recipe on page 178 for Perfect White Rice.)

3. When cook time is up, let the pressure release naturally for 2 minutes, then release the rest of the pressure manually.

4. When the pin drops, remove the lid. Remove the chicken and shred it.

5. Switch the Instant Pot to the Sauté function. Mix the cornstarch and water in a small bowl, then stir it into the liquid in the pot. Add the frozen vegetables and continue to let things simmer and stir for another 7 minutes or so.

6. Stir the chicken back into the pot and serve over cooked rice.

Ruth's Slow-Cooker Chicken

Sara Harter Fredette, Williamsburg, MA

Makes 6 servings

Prep. Time: 5 minutes ❧ Cooking Time: 6–8 hours ❧ Ideal slow-cooker size: 4-qt.

14 oz. boneless chicken thighs

10¾-oz. can condensed cream of mushroom soup

1 pkg. dry mushroom soup mix

¼–½ cup sour cream

4-oz. can mushrooms, drained

1. Combine chicken, soup, and soup mix in slow cooker.

2. Cover. Cook on Low 6–8 hours.

3. Just before serving, stir in sour cream and mushrooms. Reheat briefly.

Serving suggestions:

Serve on noodles, or Perfect White Rice on page 178.

This would also be great alongside Green Beans Caesar on page 195 or Very Special Spinach on page 194.

Wanda's Chicken and Rice Casserole

Wanda Roth, Napoleon, OH

Makes 6–8 servings
Prep. Time: 10 minutes ❧ Cooking Time: 3–4 hours ❧ Ideal slow-cooker size: 4-qt.

1 cup long-grain rice, uncooked

3 cups water

2 tsp. chicken bouillon granules

10¾-oz. can condensed cream of chicken soup

16-oz. bag frozen broccoli

2 cups chopped, cooked chicken

¼ tsp. garlic powder

1 tsp. onion salt

1 cup shredded cheddar cheese

1. Combine all ingredients in slow cooker.

2. Cook on High 3–4 hours.

Note:

If casserole is too runny, remove lid from slow cooker for 15 minutes while continuing to cook on High.

Tip:

Rotisserie chickens are cheap and easy! I use them for all of my recipes that require cooked chicken because you can't beat the price, even by making it yourself.

Spiced Lentils with Chicken and Rice

Janelle Reitz, Lancaster, PA

Makes 6 servings
Prep. Time: 10 minutes ⚬ Cooking Time: 15 minutes

I Tbsp. olive oil

3-inch cinnamon stick

¾ tsp. ground cumin

6 cloves garlic, minced

I onion, sliced

¾ lb. boneless, skinless chicken thighs, cubed

I cup uncooked brown rice, rinsed

½ cup brown lentils, rinsed

I tsp. ground cardamom

2½ cups chicken broth

½ cup raisins

2 Tbsp. chopped fresh cilantro

½ cup toasted almonds, *optional*

1. Set the Instant Pot to the Sauté function and heat the oil.

2. Sauté the cinnamon stick, cumin, and garlic for 2 minutes.

3. Add the onion and sauté until tender, about 3 to 5 minutes.

4. Press Cancel. Add the chicken, brown rice, lentils, and cardamom, in that order. Pour in the chicken broth. Do not stir.

5. Secure the lid and set the vent to sealing.

6. Manually set the cook time for 15 minutes on high pressure.

7. When the cooking time is over, let the pressure release naturally for 15 minutes, then manually release the remaining pressure.

8. When the pin drops, remove the lid. Remove the cinnamon stick. Add the raisins, cilantro, and almonds (if using).

Serving suggestion:

This would be great served alongside Vegetable Medley on page 187.

Tip:

Bouillon cubes are a cheaper way of making broth and you do not have to boil the water ahead of time. For the recipe above, simply add 2 bouillon cubes and 2½ cups of water to the inner pot. They will dissolve on their own while cooking.

One-Dish Chicken Supper

SLOW COOKER

Louise Stackhouse, Benton, PA

Makes 4 servings

Prep. Time: 5 minutes ∘ *Cooking Time: 6–8 hours* ∘ *Ideal slow-cooker size: 4-qt.*

- 24 oz. boneless, skinless chicken thighs
- 10¾-oz. can condensed cream of chicken, or celery, or mushroom, soup
- ⅓ cup milk
- 6-oz. pkg. Stove Top stuffing mix and seasoning packet
- 1⅔ cups water

1. Place chicken in slow cooker.
2. Combine soup and milk. Pour over chicken.
3. Combine stuffing mix, seasoning packet, and water. Spoon over chicken.
4. Cover. Cook on Low 6–8 hours.

Serving suggestion:
This would be great served alongside Broccoli with Garlic on page 192.

INSTANT POT

Chicken and Dumplings

Bonnie Miller, Louisville, OH

Makes 4 servings
Prep. Time: 10 minutes ⚬ Cooking Time: 3 minutes

1 Tbsp. olive oil

1 small onion, chopped

2 celery stalks, cut into 1-inch pieces

6 small carrots, cut into 1-inch chunks

2 cups chicken broth

2 lb. boneless, skinless chicken breast thighs, cut into 1-inch pieces

2 chicken bouillon cubes

1 tsp. salt

1 tsp. pepper

1 tsp. poultry seasoning

Biscuits:

2 cups buttermilk biscuit mix

½ cup plus 1 Tbsp. milk

1 tsp. parsley

1. Set the Instant Pot to the Sauté function and heat the olive oil.

2. Add the onion, celery, and carrots to the hot oil and sauté for 3 to 5 minutes.

3. Pour in the broth and scrape the bottom of the inner pot with a wooden spoon or spatula to deglaze. Press Cancel.

4. Add the chicken, bouillon, salt, pepper, and poultry seasoning.

5. Combine the biscuit ingredients in a bowl until just moistened. Drop 2-Tbsp. mounds over the contents of the inner pot, as evenly spaced out as possible.

6. Secure the lid and set the vent to sealing. Manually set the cook time for 3 minutes.

7. When the cook time is over, manually release the pressure.

Serving suggestion:
This would be great served alongside Green Beans Caesar on page 195.

Crustless Chicken Pot Pie

Hope Comerford, Clinton Township, MI

Makes 6 servings
Prep. Time: 15 minutes   Cooking Time: 30 minutes

I lb. boneless, skinless chicken thighs

3 Yukon Gold potatoes, peeled and chopped into ½-inch cubes

I cup chopped onion

2 carrots, chopped

¾ cup frozen peas

¾ cup frozen corn

½ cup chopped celery

10¾-oz. can condensed cream of chicken soup

I cup milk

I cup chicken broth

I tsp. salt

I tsp. garlic powder

I tsp. onion powder

2 Tbsp. cornstarch

2 Tbsp. cold water

16.3-oz. can flaky biscuits

1. Place all the ingredients, except for the cornstarch, water, and biscuits, into the inner pot of the Instant Pot.

2. Secure the lid and set the vent to sealing. Manually set the cook time for 25 minutes on high pressure.

3. While the Instant Pot is cooking, bake the canned biscuits according to the directions on the can.

4. When the cook time is over, manually release the pressure.

5. When the pin drops, remove the lid. Remove the chicken to a bowl. Press Cancel then press Sauté.

6. Mix together the cornstarch and water. Stir this into the contents of the Instant Pot and cook until thickened, about 5 minutes. Meanwhile, shred the chicken, then add it back in with the contents of the inner pot.

7. Serve spooned over the freshly baked flaky biscuits.

Tip:

Bouillon cubes are a cheaper way of making broth and you do not have to boil the water ahead of time. For the recipe above, simply add 1 bouillon cube and 1 cup of water to the inner pot. It will dissolve on its own while cooking.

Chicken Casablanca

Joyce Kaut, Rochester, NY

Makes 8 servings
Prep. Time: 20 minutes ❧ Cooking Time: 12 minutes

2 large onions, sliced

1 tsp. ground ginger

3 cloves garlic, minced

2 Tbsp. canola oil, *divided*

3 pounds skinless chicken pieces

3 large carrots, diced

2 large potatoes, unpeeled, diced

½ tsp. ground cumin

½ tsp. salt

½ tsp. pepper

¼ tsp. cinnamon

2 Tbsp. raisins

14½-oz. can chopped tomatoes

3 small zucchini, sliced

15-oz. can garbanzo beans, drained

2 Tbsp. chopped parsley

1. Using the Sauté function of the Instant Pot, cook the onions, ginger, and garlic in 1 Tbsp. of the oil for 5 minutes, stirring constantly. Remove onions, ginger, and garlic from pot and set aside.

2. Brown the chicken pieces with the remaining oil, then add the cooked onions, ginger and garlic back in as well as all the remaining ingredients, except the parsley.

3. Secure the lid and make sure vent is in the sealing position. Cook on Manual mode for 12 minutes.

4. When cook time is up, let the pressure release naturally for 5 minutes and then release the rest of the pressure manually.

Serving suggestion:

This would be great served alongside Cabbage and Potatoes on page 186.

Chicken Parmigiana

SLOW COOKER

Brenda Pope, Dundee, OH

Makes 6 servings

Prep. Time: 10–15 minutes ⁂ *Cooking Time: 6¼–8¼ hours* ⁂ *Ideal slow-cooker size: 4-qt.*

- 1 egg
- 1 tsp. salt
- ¼ tsp. pepper
- 24 oz. boneless, skinless chicken thighs
- 1 cup Italian breadcrumbs
- 2–4 Tbsp. butter
- 14-oz. jar pizza sauce
- 6 slices mozzarella cheese
- Grated Parmesan cheese

1. Beat egg, salt, and pepper together. Dip chicken into egg and coat with breadcrumbs. Sauté chicken in butter in skillet. Arrange chicken in slow cooker.

2. Pour pizza sauce over chicken.

3. Cover. Cook on Low 6–8 hours.

4. Layer mozzarella cheese over top and sprinkle with Parmesan cheese. Cook an additional 15 minutes.

Serving suggestion:

This would go great alongside Slow-Cooker Scalloped Potatoes on page 184 and Green Beans Caesar on page 195.

INSTANT POT

Ann's Chicken Cacciatore

Ann Driscoll, Albuquerque, NM

Makes 8 servings
Prep. Time: 25 minutes ⚶ *Cooking Time: 3–9 hours* ⚶ *Setting: Slow Cook*

1 large onion, thinly sliced

3 lb. chicken, cut up, skin removed, trimmed of fat

2 (6-oz.) cans tomato paste

4-oz. can sliced mushrooms, drained

1 tsp. salt

¼ cup dry white wine

¼ tsp. pepper

1–2 cloves garlic, minced

1–2 tsp. dried oregano

½ tsp. dried basil

½ tsp. celery seed, *optional*

1 bay leaf

1. In the inner pot of the Instant Pot, place the onion and chicken.

2. Combine remaining ingredients and pour over the chicken.

3. Secure the lid and make sure vent is at sealing. Cook on Slow Cook mode, low 7–9 hours, or high 3–4 hours. Remove bay leaf before serving.

Serving suggestion:
This would be great served alongside Perfect Pinto Beans on page 182 or Garlicky Black Beans on page 183.

Cranberry Chicken

Teena Wagner, Waterloo, ON

Makes 6–8 servings
Prep. Time: 5–10 minutes   ♣   Cooking Time: 4–8 hours   ♣   Ideal slow-cooker size: 4- to 5-qt.

3–4 lb. chicken pieces
½ tsp. salt
¼ tsp. pepper
½ cup diced celery
½ cup diced onion
16-oz. can whole berry cranberry sauce
1 cup barbecue sauce

1. Combine all ingredients in slow cooker.

2. Cover. Cook on High for 4 hours, or on Low for 6–8 hours.

Serving suggestion:

This would be great served alongside Cheesy Broccoli Rice Casserole on page 181 or Orange Glazed Carrots on page 191.

Hawaiian Chicken Tacos

Maria Shevlin, Sicklerville, NJ

Makes 8–10 servings
Prep. Time: 15 minutes ✂ *Cooking Time: 15 minutes*

6 boneless, skinless chicken thighs

20-oz. can crushed pineapple and its juice

½ cup brown sugar

2 (10¾-oz.) cans tomato soup

1 bunch green onions, chopped

Tortillas or hard taco shells, for serving

Optional Garnishes:

Sesame seeds

Shredded lettuce

Red onion

Green onion

1. Add chicken thighs to the bottom of Instant Pot inner pot and add all remaining ingredients on top.

2. Secure the lid and set the vent to sealing. Cook on the Poultry setting for 15 minutes.

3. When cook time is up, let the pressure release naturally for 5 minutes, and then manually release the remaining pressure.

4. When the pin drops, remove the lid. Shred the chicken by using 2 forks directly in the Instant Pot.

5. Add to tortillas or hard taco shells and add any or all the garnishments listed above.

Serving suggestion:

This would be great served over Perfect White Rice on page 178.

Orange-Glazed Chicken

Leona Miller, Millersburg, OH

Makes 6 servings

Prep. Time: 5 minutes & Cooking Time: 3½–9¼ hours & Ideal slow-cooker size: 4-qt.

6-oz. can frozen orange juice concentrate, thawed

½ tsp. dried marjoram

24 oz. boneless, skinless chicken thighs

¼ cup cold water

2 Tbsp. cornstarch

1. Combine orange juice and marjoram in shallow dish. Dip each breast in orange-juice mixture and place in slow cooker. Pour remaining sauce over breasts.

2. Cover. Cook on Low 7–9 hours, or on High 3¼–4 hours.

3. Remove chicken from slow cooker. Turn cooker to High and cover.

4. Combine water and cornstarch. Stir into liquid in slow cooker. Place cover slightly ajar on slow cooker. Cook until sauce is thick and bubbly, about 15–20 minutes.

Variation:

To increase "spice" in dish, add ½–1 tsp. Worcestershire sauce to orange juice marjoram glaze.

Serving suggestion:

Serve with sauce over chicken and alongside Orange Glazed Carrots on page 191.

Orange Chicken

Anita Troyer, Fairview, MI

Makes 6 servings
Prep. Time: 20 minutes ✂ *Cooking Time: 15 minutes*

2 lb. boneless skinless chicken thighs

2 Tbsp. oil

Sauce:

1 cup orange juice

1 Tbsp. grated fresh ginger

4 cloves garlic, minced

1 Tbsp. rice wine

½ cup tomato sauce

⅓ cup brown sugar

¼ cup soy sauce

Zest from an orange

2 Tbsp. orange juice

2 Tbsp. cornstarch

Serving suggestion:
Serve over Perfect White Rice on page 178 and alongside Orange Glazed Carrots on page 191.

1. Cut the chicken into 1–2-inch pieces.

2. Turn Instant Pot to Sauté. Once hot, add the oil to the inner pot. After the oil is hot, add the chicken and fry for 2–3 minutes, stirring several times. Make sure the chicken doesn't stick to the bottom of the pot.

3. Add the sauce ingredients to the chicken in the pot and stir to combine and coat chicken well.

4. Secure the lid on the pot and make sure vent is at sealing. Press the Manual function, at high pressure, for 5 minutes.

5. When cook time is up, turn off the Instant Pot and manually release the pressure.

6. Remove lid and turn pot on to Sauté.

7. Combine the orange juice and cornstarch in a small bowl and stir until well mixed. Add to pot and gently stir to combine. If stirred too vigorously, the chicken will fall apart.

8. Keep on Sauté setting until thickened, 2–3 minutes. Turn pot off.

Note:

This is even better as leftovers as the meat has time to flavor.

Wild 'N Tangy BBQ Chicken

Maria Shevlin, Sicklerville, NJ

Makes 4–6 servings
Prep. Time: 15 minutes   Cooking Time: 15 minutes

2–4 lb. boneless, skinless chicken thighs

1 cup chicken broth

1 tsp. onion powder

1 tsp. garlic powder

½–1 tsp. chili powder

¼–½ tsp. red pepper flakes

½ tsp. smoked paprika

¼ cup brown sugar

½ cup minced onion

1½ tsp. parsley flakes

2 cloves garlic, minced

18-oz. bottle of your favorite barbecue sauce

Tip:

Bouillon cubes are a cheaper way of making broth and you do not have to boil the water ahead of time. For the recipe above, simply add 1 bouillon cube and 1 cup of water to the crock. It will dissolve on its own while cooking.

1. Place all the ingredients, except the barbecue sauce, into the inner pot of the Instant Pot.

2. Secure the lid and set the vent to sealing. Manually set the cook time for 15 minutes on high pressure.

3. When cook time is up, let the pressure release naturally for 10 minutes, then manually release the remaining pressure.

4. When the pin drops, remove the lid. Carefully drain most of the broth out and reserve it.

5. Shred the chicken in the pot with your hand mixer or between 2 forks. Note: The hand mixer works like a charm!

6. Add the barbecue sauce and mix well.

7. Taste and adjust seasonings if needed. If it's too dry for your liking, add some of the reserved liquid.

Serving suggestions:

Either serve on a plate, or on slider buns with a side of coleslaw and pickles. You can also try serving it open-faced on Texas toast. This would also be great alongside Southwestern Cauliflower on page 190.

Marcy's Barbecued Chicken

Marcy Engle, Harrisonburg, VA

Makes 6 servings
Prep. Time: 5–7 minutes ⚘ *Cooking Time: 5 hours* ⚘ *Ideal slow-cooker size: 4-qt.*

2 lb. chicken pieces
¼ cup flour
1 cup ketchup
2 cups water
⅓ cup Worcestershire sauce
1 tsp. chili powder
½ tsp. salt
½ tsp. pepper
2 drops Tabasco sauce
¼ tsp. garlic salt
¼ tsp. onion salt

1. Dust chicken with flour. Transfer to slow cooker.

2. Combine remaining ingredients. Pour over chicken.

3. Cover. Cook on Low 5 hours.

Serving suggestion:

This would be great served alongside Perfect Pinto Beans on page 182 and Southwestern Cauliflower on page 190.

Turkey Sloppy Joes

Marla Folkerts, Holland, OH

Makes 6 servings
Prep. Time: 20 minutes ⚬ Cooking Time: 4 minutes

1 Tbsp. olive oil

1 red onion, chopped

1 bell pepper, chopped

1½ pounds boneless turkey, finely chopped

1 cup ketchup

½ tsp. salt

1 clove garlic, minced

1 tsp. Dijon-style mustard

⅛ tsp. pepper

6 (1½ oz. each) sandwich rolls

1. Set the Instant Pot to Sauté and add the olive oil. Once the olive oil is hot, add in the onion, pepper, and turkey. Sauté until the turkey is brown. Press Cancel.

2. Combine ketchup, salt, garlic, mustard, and pepper, then pour over the turkey mixture. Mix well.

3. Secure the lid and make sure the vent is set to sealing. Put the Instant Pot on Manual mode for 15 minutes.

4. When cook time is up, let the pressure release naturally for 5 minutes, then perform a quick release. Serve on sandwich rolls.

Tip:

You can often find frozen chopped peppers in the freezer section of your grocery store. This is often a less expensive option than fresh peppers.

Serving suggestion:

This would be great served alongside Potluck Baked Corn on page 189 and Cheesy Broccoli Rice Casserole on page 181.

Cheesy Stuffed Cabbage

Maria Shevlin, Sicklerville, NJ

Makes 6–8 servings
Prep. Time: 30 minutes ⚬ Cooking Time: 18 minutes

1–2 heads savoy cabbage
1 lb. ground turkey
1 egg
1 cup shredded cheddar cheese
2 Tbsp. heavy cream
¼ cup shredded Parmesan cheese
¼ cup shredded mozzarella cheese
¼ cup finely diced onion
¼ cup finely diced bell pepper
¼ cup finely diced mushrooms
1 tsp. salt
½ tsp. black pepper
1 tsp. garlic powder
6 basil leaves, fresh and cut chiffonade
1 Tbsp. fresh parsley, chopped
1 qt. of your favorite pasta sauce

1. Remove the core from the cabbages.

2. Boil water and place 1 head at a time into the water for approximately 10 minutes.

3. Allow cabbage to cool slightly. Once cooled, remove the leaves carefully and set aside. You'll need about 15 or 16.

4. Mix together the meat and all remaining ingredients except the pasta sauce.

5. One leaf at a time, put a heaping Tbsp. of meat mixture in the center.

6. Tuck the sides in and then roll tightly.

7. Add ½ cup sauce to the bottom of the inner pot of the Instant Pot.

8. Place the rolls, fold side down, into the pot and layer them, putting a touch of sauce between each layer and finally on top. (You may want to cook the rolls half batch at a time.)

9. Lock lid and make sure vent is at sealing. Set timer on 18 minutes on Manual at high pressure, then manually release the pressure when cook time is over.

INSTANT POT

Daddy's Pasta Fasool

Maria Shevlin, Sicklerville, NJ

Makes 8 servings
Prep. Time: 15 minutes   Cooking Time: 6 minutes

1 cup tomato sauce

1 cup diced onion

½ cup diced carrots

½ cup diced celery

1 Tbsp. chopped fresh celery leaves

14½-oz. can petite diced tomatoes

1 cup precooked ground turkey

3–4 cloves garlic, minced

1 bay leaf

½ tsp. onion powder

½ tsp. garlic powder

¼ tsp. basil

¼ tsp. oregano

½ tsp. parsley flakes

½ tsp. salt

¼ tsp. black pepper

15½-oz. can cannelini beans, rinsed and drained (I use Goya brand)

1 cup elbow pasta

4 cups chicken broth

1. In the inner pot of the Instant Pot, add the sauce, vegetables, tomatoes, meat, seasonings, and stir.

2. Set to Sauté for 5 minutes, stirring occasionally.

3. After 5 minutes add the beans, pasta, and chicken broth, in that order.

4. Lock lid, set vent to sealing, then set on Manual at high pressure for 6 minutes.

5. Release the pressure manually when cooking time is over. Remove bay leaf before serving.

Serving suggestions:

Serve topped with fresh grated Parmesan cheese and a roll with butter. This would also be great alongside Broccoli with Garlic on page 192 or Vegetable Medley on page 187.

Tip:

Bouillon cubes are a cheaper way of making broth and you do not have to boil the water ahead of time. For the recipe above, simply add 4 bouillon cubes and 4 cups of water to the inner pot. They will dissolve on their own while cooking.

Turkey Meatballs and Gravy

Betty Sue Good, Broadway, VA

Makes 10 servings

Prep. Time: 35 minutes & Cooking Time: 10 minutes

2 eggs, beaten

¾ cup breadcrumbs

½ cup finely chopped onion

½ cup finely chopped celery

2 Tbsp. chopped fresh parsley

¼ tsp. pepper

⅛ tsp. garlic powder

1½ lb. ground turkey

1½ Tbsp. canola oil

10¾-oz. can condensed cream of mushroom soup

1 cup water

⅞-oz. package turkey gravy mix

½ tsp. dried thyme

2 bay leaves

1. Combine eggs, breadcrumbs, onion, celery, parsley, pepper, garlic powder, and meat. Shape into ¾-inch balls.

2. Set the Instant Pot to Sauté and add in the oil. Lightly brown meatballs in the oil in as many batches as needed. As the meatballs are browned, let them drain on a paper towel–lined plate or dish, then pat dry.

3. When all the meatballs are browned, press Cancel on the Instant Pot and then wipe out the inside of the inner pot. Place the meatballs back inside.

4. Combine soup, water, dry gravy mix, thyme, and bay leaves in a bowl, then pour over the meatballs.

5. Secure the lid and make sure the vent is set to sealing. Press the Manual button and set for 10 minutes.

6. When cook time is up, let the pressure release naturally. Discard bay leaves before serving.

Tips:

1. If you don't have breadcrumbs, you can crush up saltine crackers and use those instead.

2. You do not have to use ground turkey for this recipe. If ground beef is what's on sale, you may use that instead.

Serving suggestions:

Serve over mashed potatoes or buttered noodles. This would also be great alongside Green Beans Caesar on page 195.

Turkey Meat Loaf

Delores A. Gnagey, Saginaw, MI

Makes 4–5 servings

Prep. Time: 15 minutes ❧ Cooking Time: 15 minutes ❧ Standing Time: 10 minutes

I cup plus I Tbsp. water, *divided*

I lb. lean ground turkey

½ small onion, minced

I ½ Tbsp. minced fresh parsley

2 eggs, whites only

2 Tbsp. milk

½ tsp. dry mustard

¼ tsp. salt

⅛ tsp. ground white pepper

Pinch nutmeg

I slice bread, lightly toasted, made into coarse crumbs

I Tbsp. ketchup

Tip:

You do not have to use ground turkey for this recipe. If ground beef is what's on sale, you may use that instead.

Serving suggestion:

This would be great served alongside Potluck Baked Corn on page 189 and Southwestern Cauliflower on page 190.

1. Set the trivet inside the inner pot of the Instant Pot and pour in 1 cup water.

2. In a medium bowl, mix the ground turkey, onion, and parsley. Set aside.

3. In another bowl, whisk the egg whites. Add the milk, mustard, salt, pepper, and nutmeg to the egg. Whisk to blend.

4. Add the breadcrumbs to the egg mixture. Let rest 10 minutes.

5. Add the egg mixture to the meat mixture and blend well.

6. Spray the inside of a 7-inch springform baking pan, then spread the meat mixture into it.

7. Blend together the ketchup and 1 Tbsp. water in a small bowl. Spread the mixture on top of the meat. Cover the pan with aluminum foil.

8. Place the springform pan on top of the trivet inside the inner pot.

9. Secure the lid and set the vent to sealing.

10. Manually set the cook time for 15 minutes on high pressure.

11. When the cooking time is over, let the pressure release naturally.

12. When the pin drops, remove the lid and use oven mitts to carefully remove the trivet from the inner pot.

13. Allow the meat to stand 10 minutes before slicing to serve.

Turkey Loaf

Dottie Schmidt, Kansas City, MO

Makes 5–6 servings
Prep. Time: 15 minutes ❧ Cooking Time: 3–4 hours ❧ Ideal slow-cooker size: 4- or 5-qt.

1 ¼ lb. ground turkey
½ cup dry breadcrumbs
½ cup finely chopped celery
1 egg, beaten
2 green onions, finely chopped
¼ tsp. salt
⅛ tsp. black pepper
1 Tbsp. Worcestershire sauce
2 Tbsp. ketchup
1–2 Tbsp. sesame seeds

Tip:

You do not have to use ground turkey for this recipe. If ground beef is what's on sale, you may use that instead.

Serving suggestion:

This would be great served alongside Potluck Baked Corn on page 189 and Southwestern Cauliflower on page 190.

1. Grease interior of slow-cooker crock.

2. Make a tin foil sling for your slow cooker so you can lift the cooked Turkey Loaf out easily. Begin by folding a strip of tin foil accordion-fashion so that it's about 1½–2 inches wide, and long enough to fit from the top edge of the crock, down inside and up the other side, plus a 2-inch overhang on each side of the cooker. Make a second strip exactly like the first.

3. Place the one strip in the crock, running from end to end. Place the second strip in the crock, running from side to side. The two strips should form a cross in the bottom of the crock.

4. Combine all ingredients except ketchup and sesame seeds in bowl, mixing gently but well.

5. Form into 6-inch-long loaf and place in crock, centering loaf where foil strips cross.

6. Spread ketchup over top of loaf. Sprinkle with sesame seeds.

7. Cover. Cook on Low for 3–4 hours, or until instant-read meat thermometer registers 150°–155° when stuck in center of loaf.

8. Using foil handles, lift loaf out of crock and onto cutting board. Cover and keep warm for 10 minutes. Then slice and serve.

Pork

Pork Chops with Potatoes and Green Beans

Hope Comerford, Clinton Township, MI

Makes 4 servings
Prep. Time: 8 minutes   ⚮   Cooking Time: 13 minutes

2 Tbsp. olive oil, *divided*

4 bone-in pork chops,
1–1½ inches thick

Salt and pepper to taste

1 cup chicken broth

2 lb. baby potatoes, sliced in half

1 lb. fresh green beans, end trimmed

3 cloves garlic, crushed

2 tsp. salt

1 tsp. onion powder

1 tsp. dried rosemary

½ tsp. dried thyme

¼ tsp. pepper

1. Set the Instant Pot to Sauté and let it get hot. Add 1 Tbsp. of the oil.

2. Sprinkle each side of the pork chops with salt and pepper. Brown them on each side in the Instant Pot. Remove them when done.

3. Pour in the broth and scrape the bottom of the pot, bringing up any stuck-on bits. Press Cancel.

4. Arrange the pork chops back in the inner pot of the Instant Pot.

5. In a medium bowl, toss the potatoes and green beans with the garlic, salt, onion powder, rosemary, thyme, and pepper. Pour them over the pork chops.

6. Secure the lid and set the vent to sealing. Manually set the cook time for 8 minutes on high pressure.

7. When cook time is up, let the pressure release naturally for 10 minutes, then manually release the remaining pressure.

Tip:

Bouillon cubes are a cheaper way of making broth and you do not have to boil the water ahead of time. For the recipe above, simply add 1 bouillon cube and 1 cup of water to the inner pot. It will dissolve on its own while cooking.

Paprika Pork Chops with Rice

Sharon Easter, Yuba City, CA

Makes 4 servings
Prep. Time: 5 minutes   Cooking Time: 30 minutes

⅛ tsp. pepper

1 tsp. paprika

4–5 thick-cut bone-in pork chops (1–1½ inches thick)

1 Tbsp. olive oil

1¼ cups water, *divided*

1 onion, sliced

½ green bell pepper, sliced in rings

1½ cups canned stewed tomatoes

1 cup brown rice

Serving suggestion:

This would be great served alongside Vegetable Medley on page 187 or Broccoli with Garlic on page 192.

1. Mix the pepper and paprika in a flat dish. Dredge the chops in the seasoning mixture.

2. Set the Instant Pot to the Sauté function and heat the oil in the inner pot.

3. Brown the chops on both sides for 1 to 2 minutes a side. Remove the pork chops and set aside.

4. Pour a small amount of water into the inner pot and scrape up any bits from the bottom with a wooden spoon. Press Cancel.

5. Place the browned chops side by side in the inner pot. Place 1 slice onion and 1 ring of green pepper on top of each chop. Spoon tomatoes with their juices over the top.

6. Pour the rice in and pour the remaining water over the top.

7. Secure the lid and set the vent to sealing.

8. Manually set the cook time for 30 minutes on high pressure.

9. When the cooking time is over, manually release the pressure.

Tangy Pork Chops

SLOW COOKER

Tracy Clark, Mt. Crawford, VA
Lois M. Martin, Lititz, PA
Becky Oswald, Broadway, PA

Makes 4 servings
Prep. Time: 15 minutes   *Cooking Time: 5½–6½ hours*   *Ideal slow-cooker size: 4-qt.*

4 ½-inch-thick pork chops
½ tsp. salt
⅛ tsp. pepper
2 medium onions, chopped
2 celery ribs, chopped
I large green pepper, sliced
14½-oz. can stewed tomatoes
½ cup ketchup
2 Tbsp. cider vinegar
2 Tbsp. brown sugar
2 Tbsp. Worcestershire sauce
I Tbsp. lemon juice
I beef bouillon cube
2 Tbsp. cornstarch
2 Tbsp. water

1. Place chops in slow cooker. Sprinkle with salt and pepper.

2. Add onions, celery, pepper, and tomatoes.

3. Combine ketchup, vinegar, brown sugar, Worcestershire sauce, lemon juice, and bouillon cube. Pour over vegetables.

4. Cover. Cook on Low 5–6 hours.

5. Combine cornstarch and water until smooth. Stir into slow cooker.

6. Cover. Cook on High 30 minutes, or until thickened.

Serving suggestion:

Serve over Perfect White Rice on page 178 and with Very Special Spinach on page 194.

Variation:

Use chunks of beef or chicken legs and thighs instead of pork.

Saucy Pork Chops

Bonita Ensenberger, Albuquerque, NM

Makes 4 servings
Prep. Time: 15–20 minutes ❦ Cooking Time: 4–9 hours ❦ Ideal slow-cooker size: 4-qt.

4 pork chops

Salt and pepper to taste

1 tsp. garlic powder

1 Tbsp. oil

2–2½ cups ketchup

½ cup brown sugar

1 Tbsp. hickory-flavored liquid smoke

1 cup chopped onion

1. Season chops with salt, pepper, and garlic powder. Brown on both sides in oil in skillet. Drain.

2. Combine ketchup, brown sugar, and liquid smoke in bowl.

3. Place onion in slow cooker. Dip browned pork chops in sauce mixture and place on onion. Pour remaining sauce over chops.

4. Cover. Cook on Low 7–9 hours, or on High 4–5 hours.

Serving suggestion:

Makes a great meal served with coleslaw, or alongside Wild Rice on page 179 and Southwestern Cauliflower on page 190.

Pork Chops in Gravy

Hope Comerford, Clinton Township, MI

Makes 6 servings
Prep. Time: 10 minutes ⚬ Cooking Time: 20 minutes

1 Tbsp. olive oil

½ cup sliced onion

6 bone-in pork chops,
1–1½ inches thick

Salt and pepper to taste

1½ cups beef broth, *divided*

1 tsp. Worcestershire sauce

½ tsp. soy sauce

1 tsp. garlic powder

1 tsp. onion powder

2 tsp. cornstarch

2 tsp. cold water

½ cup sour cream

Tip:

Bouillon cubes are a cheaper way of making broth. For the recipe above, simply add 1–2 bouillon cubes to 1½ cups of hot water to make the broth.

1. Set the Instant Pot to Sauté and let it get hot. Add the oil.

2. Sauté the onion for 3 minutes.

3. Sprinkle each side of the pork chops with salt and pepper. Brown 3 of them at a time on each side in the Instant Pot. Remove them when done.

4. Pour in ½ cup of the broth and scrape the bottom of the pot, bringing up any stuck-on bits. Press Cancel.

5. Arrange the pork chops in the inner pot of the Instant Pot.

6. Pour the remaining broth, Worcestershire sauce, soy sauce, garlic powder, and onion powder over the chops.

7. Secure the lid and set the vent to sealing. Manually set the cook time for 8 minutes on high pressure.

8. When the cook time is over, let the pressure release naturally for 10 minutes, then manually release the remaining pressure.

9. When the pin drops, remove the lid. Switch the Instant Pot to Sauté.

10. Remove the chops and set aside.

11. Mix the cornstarch and cold water, then whisk into the sauce in the pot. Let thicken slightly for a few minutes. Press Cancel.

12. Before you add the sour cream to the sauce, let it cool for a few minutes, then slowly whisk it in. Serve the chops with the gravy over the top.

Pork Chops and Gravy

Sharon Wantland, Menomonee Falls, WI

Makes 8 servings
Prep. Time: 10 minutes   Cooking Time: 3–8 hours   Ideal slow-cooker size: 6-qt.

8 pork chops

Salt and pepper to taste

2 Tbsp. oil

2 (10¾-oz.) cans condensed cream of mushroom soup

1 large onion, sliced

12-oz. can evaporated milk

1. Season pork chops with salt and pepper. Brown in oil. Drain. Transfer to slow cooker.

2. In separate bowl, whisk together mushroom soup, onion, and evaporated milk until smooth. Pour over chops.

3. Cook on High 3–4 hours, or on Low 6–8 hours.

Variation:

To increase flavor, stir ½–1 cup sour cream, or ¼ cup sherry, into mixture during last 30 minutes of cooking time.

Serving suggestion:

This would be great served alongside Potluck Baked Corn on page 189.

Pork Chops in Bean Sauce

Shirley Sears, Tiskilwa, IL

Makes 6 servings

Prep. Time: 15–20 minutes ⚬ *Cooking Time: 7–8 hours* ⚬ *Ideal slow-cooker size: 5-qt.*

6 pork chops

⅓ cup chopped onion

½ tsp. salt

⅓ tsp. garlic salt

⅛ tsp. pepper

28-oz. can baked beans

¼ tsp. hot pepper sauce

13½-oz. can crushed pineapple, undrained

⅓ cup chili sauce

1. Brown pork chops in skillet five minutes per side. Place in slow cooker.

2. Sauté onion in skillet in meat juices. Spread over pork chops.

3. Sprinkle with salt, garlic salt, and pepper.

4. Combine beans and hot sauce. Pour over chops.

5. Combine pineapple and chili sauce. Spread evenly over beans.

6. Cover. Cook on Low 7–8 hours.

Serving suggestion:

This would be great served alongside Orange Glazed Carrots on page 191 and Wild Rice on page 179.

INSTANT POT

BBQ Pork Sandwiches

Carol Eveleth, Cheyenne, WY

Makes 4 servings
Prep. Time: 20 minutes   Cooking Time: 60 minutes

2 tsp. salt

1 tsp. onion powder

1 tsp. garlic powder

2-lb. pork shoulder roast, cut into 3-inch pieces

1 Tbsp. olive oil

2 cups barbecue sauce

1. In a small bowl, combine the salt, onion powder, and garlic powder. Season the pork with the rub.

2. Turn the Instant Pot on to Sauté. Heat the olive oil in the inner pot.

3. Add the pork to the oil and turn to coat. Lock the lid and set vent to sealing.

4. Press Manual and cook on high pressure for 45 minutes.

5. When cooking is complete, release the pressure manually, then open the lid.

6. Using 2 forks, shred the pork, pour barbecue sauce over the pork, then press Sauté. Simmer, 3 to 5 minutes. Press Cancel. Toss pork to mix.

Serving suggestions:

Pile the shredded pork on the bottom half of a bun. Add any additional toppings if you wish, then finish with the top half of the bun.

Serve alongside Perfect Pinto Beans on page 182 and Southwestern Cauliflower on page 190.

Beef

Mississippi Pot Roast

Hope Comerford, Clinton Township, MI

Makes 8 servings
Prep. Time: 10–12 minutes 🍴 Cooking Time: 60 minutes

2 Tbsp. olive oil

3–4-lb. chuck or sirloin roast
(cut into large chunks to fit the
Instant Pot if necessary)

½ cup beef broth

1-oz. pkg. dry ranch seasoning

1-oz. pkg. au jus gravy mix

16-oz. jar sliced pepperoncini,
with juice

Tip:

If you are pressed for time,
you can skip the sauté step,
but it is highly recommended.

1. Set the Instant Pot to the Sauté setting and heat the olive oil. Sear the chuck roast on all sides. This will take 8 to 10 minutes.

2. Remove the roast and set aside. Pour in the beef broth and scrape the bottom of the inner pot with a wooden spoon or spatula to scrape up any bits. Press Cancel.

3. Place the roast back in the inner pot and sprinkle with the ranch seasoning and au jus gravy mix. Pour the jar of pepperoncini over the top, including the juices.

4. Secure the lid and set the vent to sealing. Manually set the cook time for 60 minutes on high pressure.

5. When the cook time is over, let the pressure release naturally for 15 minutes, then manually release the remaining pressure.

6. When the pin drops, remove the roast and shred between 2 forks. Discard any large pieces of fat.

7. Skim off as much fat from the juice in the inner pot as possible, then stir the shredded roast back through.

Serving suggestions:

Serve over mashed potatoes. This is also delicious served on sub rolls with melted cheese on top, or as open-faced sandwiches.

SLOW COOKER

Paul's Beef Bourguignonne

Janice Muller, Derwood, MD

Makes 4 servings
Prep. Time: 10 minutes ⚜ *Marinating Time: 6–14 hours*
Cooking Time: 8–10 hours ⚜ *Ideal slow-cooker size: 4-qt.*

3-lb. chuck or sirloin roast, cubed

2 Tbsp. oil

2 (10¾-oz.) cans golden cream of mushroom soup

1 pkg. dry onion soup mix

1 cup cooking sherry

1. Brown meat in oil in skillet. Drain. Place in slow cooker. Add remaining ingredients and cover.

2. Refrigerate 6–8 hours, or up to 14 hours, to marinate.

3. Remove from refrigerator, cover, and cook on Low 8–10 hours.

Serving suggestion:

Serve over cooked egg noodles or Perfect White Rice on page 178. This would also be great alongside Southwestern Cauliflower on page 190.

Chuck Wagon Beef

Charlotte Bull, Cassville, MO

Makes 8 servings

Prep. Time: 20 minutes ⚶ Cooking Time: 8¼–10¼ hours ⚶ Ideal slow-cooker size: 4-qt.

4-lb. boneless chuck or sirloin roast

1 tsp. garlic salt

¼ tsp. black pepper

2 Tbsp. oil

6–8 cloves garlic, minced

1 large onion, sliced

1 cup water

1 beef bouillon cube

2–3 tsp. instant coffee

1 bay leaf, or 1 Tbsp. mixed Italian herbs

3 Tbsp. cold water

2 Tbsp. cornstarch

1. Sprinkle roast with garlic salt and pepper. Brown on all sides in oil in saucepan. Place in slow cooker.

2. Sauté garlic and onion in meat drippings in saucepan. Add water, bouillon cube, and coffee. Cook over low heat for several minutes, stirring until drippings loosen. Pour over meat in cooker.

3. Add bay leaf or herbs.

4. Cover. Cook on Low 8–10 hours, or until very tender. Remove bay leaf and discard. Remove meat to serving platter and keep warm.

5. Mix water and cornstarch together until paste forms. Stir into hot liquid and onion in cooker. Cover. Cook 10 minutes on High, or until thickened.

Serving suggestions:

Slice meat and serve with gravy over top or on the side. This would also be great served alongside Wild Rice on page 179 and Green Beans Caesar on page 195.

Beef Stroganoff

Julette Leaman, Harrisonburg, VA

Makes 6 servings

Prep. Time: 15 minutes ❧ Cooking Time: 6–8 hours ❧ Ideal slow-cooker size: 3½-qt.

2 lb. ground beef

2 medium onions, chopped

2 cloves garlic, minced

6½-oz. can mushrooms

1½ cups sour cream

4 Tbsp. flour

2½ tsp. salt

¼ tsp. pepper

1 cup beef broth

3 Tbsp. tomato paste

1. In skillet, brown beef, onions, garlic, and mushrooms until meat and onions are brown. Drain. Pour into slow cooker.

2. Combine sour cream and flour. Add to mixture in slow cooker. Stir in remaining ingredients.

3. Cover. Cook on Low 6–8 hours.

Serving suggestion:

Serve over hot buttered noodles and alongside Broccoli with Garlic on page 192.

10-Layer Slow-Cooker Dish

Norma Saltzman, Shickley, NE

Makes 6–8 servings
Prep. Time: 20 minutes ❧ Cooking Time: 4 hours ❧ Ideal slow-cooker size: 5-qt.

6 medium potatoes, thinly sliced

I medium onion, thinly sliced

Salt and pepper to taste

15-oz. can corn

15-oz. can peas

¼ cup water

1½ lb. ground beef, browned

10¾-oz. can cream of mushroom soup

Serving suggestion:
This would be great served alongside Potluck Baked Corn on page 189.

Layer the ingredients in slow cooker as follows:

1. Layer 1: ¼ of potatoes, ½ of onion, salt, and pepper.

2. Layer 2: ½ can of corn.

3. Layer 3: ¼ of potatoes.

4. Layer 4: ½ can of peas.

5. Layer 5: ¼ of potatoes, ½ of onion, salt, and pepper.

6. Layer 6: remaining corn.

7. Layer 7: remaining potatoes.

8. Layer 8: remaining peas and water.

9. Layer 9: ground beef.

10. Layer 10: soup.

11. Cover. Cook on High 4 hours.

Meal-In-One-Casserole

Elizabeth Yoder, Millersburg, OH
Marcella Stalter, Flanagan, IL

Makes 4–6 servings
Prep. Time: 20 minutes ☙ Cooking Time: 4 hours ☙ Ideal slow-cooker size: 4-qt.

1 lb. ground beef
1 medium onion, chopped
1 medium green pepper, chopped
15¼-oz. can whole kernel corn, drained
4-oz. can mushrooms, drained
1 tsp. salt
¼ tsp. pepper
11-oz. jar salsa
5 cups uncooked medium egg noodles
28-oz. can diced tomatoes, undrained
1 cup shredded cheddar cheese

1. Cook beef and onion in saucepan over medium heat until meat is no longer pink. Drain. Transfer to slow cooker.

2. Top with green pepper, corn, and mushrooms. Sprinkle with salt and pepper. Pour salsa over mushrooms. Cover and cook on Low 3 hours.

3. Cook noodles according to package in separate pan. Drain and add to slow cooker after mixture in cooker has cooked for 3 hours. Top with tomatoes. Sprinkle with cheese.

4. Cover. Cook on Low 1 more hour.

Variation:

Add uncooked noodles after salsa. Pour tomatoes and 1 cup water over contents of crock. Sprinkle with cheese. Cover and cook on Low 4 hours, or until noodles are tender.

Beef and Zucchini Casserole

Judi Manos, West Islip, NY

Makes 6 servings

Prep. Time: 12 minutes   Cooking Time: 22 minutes

2 tsp. canola oil

½ cup finely chopped onion

1 lb. ground beef

1 lb. (3 small) zucchini, cut into
¼-inch-thick slices

¼ lb. fresh mushrooms, sliced

14½-oz. can diced tomatoes

½ tsp. garlic powder

½ tsp. dried oregano

1 cup brown rice

2 cups water

¼ cup grated Parmesan cheese

1. Set the Instant Pot to Sauté and heat the oil in the inner pot.

2. Sauté the onion for about 3 minutes, then add the ground beef and sauté for about 8 more minutes, or until the beef is no longer pink.

3. Press Cancel. Add the remaining ingredients, except for the grated Parmesan cheese, into the inner pot in the order shown.

4. Secure the lid and set the vent to sealing.

5. Manually set the cook time for 22 minutes on high pressure.

6. When the cooking time is over, let the pressure release naturally.

7. When the pin drops, remove the lid, and stir in the Parmesan cheese. Serve and enjoy!

SLOW COOKER

Swedish Cabbage Rolls

Jean Butzer, Batavia, NY
Pam Hochstedler, Kalona, IA

Makes 6 servings
Prep. Time: 25 minutes   Cooking Time: 7–9 hours   Ideal slow-cooker size: 2- to 4-qt.

12 large cabbage leaves
1 egg, beaten
¼ cup milk
¼ cup finely chopped onion
1 tsp. salt
¼ tsp. pepper
1 lb. ground beef, browned and drained
1 cup cooked rice
8-oz. can tomato sauce
1 Tbsp. brown sugar
1 Tbsp. lemon juice
1 tsp. Worcestershire sauce

1. Immerse cabbage leaves in boiling water for about 3 minutes or until limp. Drain.

2. Combine egg, milk, onion, salt, pepper, beef, and rice. Place about ¼ cup meat mixture in center of each leaf. Fold in sides and roll ends over meat. Place in slow cooker.

3. Combine tomato sauce, brown sugar, lemon juice, and Worcestershire sauce. Pour over cabbage rolls.

4. Cover. Cook on Low 7–9 hours.

Serving suggestion:

This would be great served alongside Broccoli with Garlic on page 192.

Helen's Lasagna

Helen King, Fairbank, IA
Clarice Williams, Fairbank, IA
Nancy Zimmerman, Loysville, PA

Makes 6–8 servings
Prep. Time: 20 minutes ⚬ Cooking Time: 4–5 hours ⚬ Ideal slow-cooker size: 6-qt.

I lb. ground beef

I medium onion, chopped

2 cloves garlic, minced

29-oz. can tomato sauce

I cup water

6-oz. can tomato paste

I tsp. salt

I tsp. dried oregano

8-oz. pkg. lasagna noodles, uncooked

4 cups (32 oz.) shredded mozzarella cheese

1½ cups (12 oz.) small-curd cottage cheese

½ cup grated Parmesan cheese

1. Cook beef, onion, and garlic together in saucepan until browned. Drain.

2. Stir in tomato sauce, water, tomato paste, salt, and oregano. Mix well.

3. Spread one-fourth of meat sauce in ungreased slow cooker. Arrange one-third of noodles over sauce.

4. Combine the cheeses. Spoon one-third of cheese mixture over noodles. Repeat layers twice. Top with remaining meat sauce.

5. Cover. Cook on Low 4–5 hours.

Variation:

For a fuller flavor, use 14-oz. can tomato sauce instead of 6-oz. can tomato paste and water. Add ½ tsp. garlic powder, 1 tsp. dried basil, and ¼ tsp. pepper.

Serving suggestion:

This would be great served alongside Green Beans Caesar on page 195 or Broccoli with Garlic on page 192.

Tamale Pie

Jeannine Janzen, Elbing, KS

Makes 8 servings
Prep. Time: 10 minutes ❖ Cooking Time: 4 hours ❖ Ideal slow-cooker size: 4-qt.

¾ cup cornmeal

1½ cups milk

1 egg, beaten

1 lb. ground beef, browned and drained

1 pkg. dry chili seasoning mix

16-oz. can diced tomatoes

16-oz. can corn, drained

1 cup grated cheddar cheese

1. Combine cornmeal, milk, and egg.

2. Stir in meat, chili seasoning mix, tomatoes, and corn until well blended. Pour into slow cooker.

3. Cover. Cook on High 1 hour, then on Low 3 hours.

4. Sprinkle with cheese. Cook another 5 minutes until cheese is melted.

Serving suggestion:

This would be great served alongside Potluck Baked Corn on page 189.

INSTANT POT

Taco Meat

Hope Comerford, Clinton Township, MI

Makes 8 servings
Prep. Time: 10 minutes ⚶ Cooking Time: 20–25 minutes

1 Tbsp. olive oil

1 large, sweet onion, chopped

2 lb. ground sirloin

2 Tbsp. chili powder

1 Tbsp. cumin

2½ tsp. garlic powder

2½ tsp. onion powder

1 tsp. salt

½ tsp. oregano

½ tsp. red pepper flakes

2 Tbsp. water

1. Set the Instant Pot to the Sauté function. Let it get hot. Add the oil.

2. Sauté the onion for 3 minutes. Add the beef and seasonings to the inner pot and sauté until browned, about 5 minutes.

3. Add the water and scrape the bottom of the pot to bring up any stuck-on bits. Press Cancel.

4. Secure the lid and set the vent to sealing. Manually set the cook time for 15 minutes on high pressure.

5. When cook time is up, manually release the pressure. When the pin drops, remove the lid.

6. Switch the Instant Pot back to Sauté and cook off the excess liquid for 5–10 minutes.

Serving suggestions:

Serve in your favorite hard or soft taco shells and with your favorite toppings.
    This would also be great served alongside Southwestern Cauliflower on page 190 and Garlicky Black Beans on page 183.

Taco Bake

Shelia Heil, Lancaster, PA

Makes 4–6 servings

Prep. Time: 10–15 minutes & *Cooking Time: 1½–4 hours* & *Ideal slow-cooker size: 4-qt.*

1 lb. ground beef
1 onion, chopped
¾ cup water
15-oz. can tomato sauce
1¼-oz. pkg. taco seasoning
8-oz. pkg. shell macaroni, uncooked

1. Brown beef and onion in a skillet.

2. Drain off drippings.

3. Add water, tomato sauce, and taco seasoning.

4. Mix well.

5. Simmer 15 minutes in skillet.

6. Transfer to slow cooker.

7. Stir in uncooked macaroni.

8. Cover. Cook on High 1½ hours, or on Low 4 hours, or until macaroni are fully cooked but not mushy.

Serving suggestions:

Just before serving, top with shredded cheddar cheese. This would also be great served alongside Perfect Pinto Beans on page 182.

Enchilada Stack-Up

Sally Holzem, Schofield, WI

Makes 8 servings

Prep. Time: 30 minutes ⚜ *Cooking Time: 4–5 hours* ⚜ *Ideal slow-cooker size: 5-qt.*

1 lb. ground beef

1 cup chopped onion

½ cup chopped red, yellow, or orange bell peppers

1 tsp. olive oil

15-oz. can kidney beans, rinsed and drained

15-oz. can black beans, rinsed and drained

14½-oz. can diced tomatoes and green chilies

1½ tsp. cumin

¼ tsp. black pepper

6 (8-inch) tortillas

2 cups shredded cheddar cheese

Serving suggestion:

This would be great served alongside Potluck Baked Corn on page 189.

1. Cut 3 (25 × 3-inch) strips of heavy-duty foil. Crisscross strips so they resemble spokes of a wheel inside bottom and up sides of crock. Spray with cooking spray.

2. In skillet, brown ground beef, onion, and bell peppers in olive oil.

3. Drain off drippings and discard.

4. Stir black beans, kidney beans, tomatoes, cumin, and black pepper into beef-veggie mixture in skillet.

5. Lay 1 tortilla in bottom of crock (and over top of the foil strips). Spoon ¾ cup bean mixture over top. Sprinkle with ⅓ of cheese.

6. Repeat layers 5 times.

7. Cover and cook on Low 4–5 hours, until very hot in the middle.

8. Use foil strips as handles to remove stack from slow cooker to platter.

9. Gently ease foil strips out from underneath stack, or bend them over so they're out of the way.

10. Cover stack to keep warm. Allow to stand 10–15 minutes to firm up. Then cut into wedges and serve.

Sloppy Joes

Nadine Martinitz, Salina, KS

Makes 6 servings

Prep. Time: 10–15 minutes ⚬ *Cooking Time: 2–6 hours* ⚬ *Ideal slow-cooker size: 4- to 5-qt.*

1 lb. ground beef
1 small onion, chopped
1 small green pepper, chopped
14½-oz. can diced tomatoes
3 Tbsp. brown sugar
2 tsp. Worcestershire sauce
1½ tsp. ground cumin
1 tsp. chili powder
½ tsp. salt

1. Brown beef in skillet, stirring to break into small pieces.

2. Add onion and pepper to meat in skillet, cooking a few more minutes. Drain off drippings.

3. Transfer meat mixture to slow cooker.

4. Stir in tomatoes, brown sugar, Worcestershire sauce, and seasonings.

5. Cover and cook until flavors are well blended, 2 hours on High or 6 hours on Low.

Serving suggestions:

To serve, fill each hamburger bun with ½ cup beef mixture. This would be great served alongside Very Special Spinach on page 194 and Perfect Pinto Beans on page 182.

Coney Dogs

Anita Troyer, Fairview, MI

Makes 8 servings
Prep. Time: 30 minutes   ❧   Cooking Time: 3 hours   ❧   Ideal slow-cooker size: 4-qt.

1½ lb. ground beef

1½ cups diced onion

1 clove garlic, crushed

2 Tbsp. chili powder

1 Tbsp. prepared mustard

16-oz. can tomato sauce

½ cup water

2 lb. hot dogs, or smoked sausage, cut into 5-inch lengths

Hot dog rolls or cooked pasta

1. Grease interior of slow-cooker crock.

2. If you have time, brown beef, onion, and garlic together in a skillet.

3. When browned, place in crock.

4. If you're using fresh sausage, brown in drippings in skillet. Place in crock.

5. Stir chili powder, mustard, tomato sauce, and water into meat in crock. Mix well.

6. Cover. Cook on Low for 2 hours.

7. Stir in hot dogs or fresh sausage. Cook on Low another hour, uncovered so sauce can reduce.

8. Serve in rolls or over pasta.

Serving suggestion:

This would be great served alongside Perfect Pinto Beans on page 182 and Potluck Baked Corn on page 189.

Meatless & Seafood

Meatless Ziti

Hope Comerford, Clinton Township, MI

Makes 8 servings
Prep. Time: 10 minutes ❧ *Cooking Time: 3 minutes*

1 Tbsp. olive oil
1 small onion, chopped
3 cups water, *divided*
15-oz. can crushed tomatoes
8-oz. can tomato sauce
1½ tsp. Italian seasoning
1 tsp. garlic powder
1 tsp. onion powder
1 tsp. sea salt
¼ tsp. pepper
12 oz. ziti
1–2 cups shredded mozzarella cheese

Serving suggestion:
This would be great served alongside Broccoli with Garlic on page 192 or Green Beans Caesar on page 195.

1. Set the Instant Pot to the Sauté function and heat the olive oil.

2. When the oil is hot, sauté the onion for 3 to 5 minutes, or until translucent.

3. Pour in 1 cup of the water and scrape any bits from the bottom of the inner pot with a wooden spoon or spatula.

4. In a bowl, mix the crushed tomatoes, tomato sauce, Italian seasoning, garlic powder, onion powder, sea salt, and pepper. Pour 1 cup of this in the inner pot and stir.

5. Pour in the ziti. Press it down so it's in there evenly, but do not stir.

6. Pour the remaining pasta sauce evenly over the top. Again, do not stir.

7. Secure the lid and set the vent to sealing. Manually set the cook time for 3 minutes.

8. When the cook time is over, let the pressure release naturally for 10 minutes, then manually release the remaining pressure.

9. When the pin drops, remove the lid and stir in the shredded mozzarella. This will thicken as it sits a bit.

Fresh Veggie Lasagna

Deanne Gingrich, Lancaster, PA

Makes 4–6 servings
Prep. Time: 30 minutes ❧ Cooking Time: 4 hours ❧ Ideal slow-cooker size: 4- or 5-qt.

1½ cups shredded mozzarella cheese

½ cup ricotta cheese

⅓ cup grated Parmesan cheese

1 egg, lightly beaten

1 tsp. dried oregano

¼ tsp. garlic powder

3 cups marinara sauce, *divided*, plus more for serving

1 medium zucchini, diced, *divided*

4 uncooked lasagna noodles

4 cups fresh baby spinach, *divided*

1 cup fresh mushrooms, sliced, *divided*

Variation:

You may use small curd cottage cheese in place of the ricotta, as it usually tends to be less expensive.

Serving suggestion:

This would be great served alongside Vegetable Medley on page 187.

1. Grease interior of slow-cooker crock.

2. In a bowl, mix together mozzarella, ricotta and Parmesan cheeses, egg, oregano, and garlic powder. Set aside.

3. Spread ½ cup marinara sauce in crock.

4. Sprinkle with half the zucchini.

5. Spoon ⅓ of cheese mixture over zucchini.

6. Break 2 noodles into large pieces to cover cheese layer.

7. Spread ½ cup marinara over noodles.

8. Top with half the spinach and then half the mushrooms.

9. Repeat layers, ending with cheese mixture, and then sauce. Press layers down firmly.

10. Cover. Cook on Low 4 hours, or until vegetables are as tender as you like them and noodles are fully cooked.

11. Let stand 15 minutes so lasagna can firm up before serving.

Easy Spinach Lasagna

LaRee Eby, Portland, OR

Makes 6–8 servings
Prep. Time: 30 minutes ⚜ Cooking Time: 4–4½ hours ⚜ Chilling Time: 8 hours or overnight
Standing Time: 15 minutes ⚜ Ideal slow-cooker size: 5- or 6-qt.

28-oz. jar spaghetti sauce

8-oz. can tomato sauce

¼ cup water

1 tsp. dried basil

1 tsp. dried oregano

¾ lb. fresh spinach, chopped, lightly steamed and squeezed dry, or 10-oz. box frozen chopped spinach, thawed and squeezed dry

16-oz. container cottage cheese

1 egg, slightly beaten

¼ tsp. black pepper (coarsely ground is best)

8 oz. uncooked lasagna noodles

2 cups (8 oz.) grated mozzarella cheese, *divided*

½ cup grated Parmesan cheese

Variations:

1. Add a chopped onion to Step 1.

2. Add 1 tsp. salt to Step 1.

Serving suggestion:
This would be great served alongside Vegetable Medley on page 187.

1. Grease interior of slow-cooker crock.

2. In large bowl, mix together spaghetti sauce, tomato sauce, water, basil, oregano, and spinach.

3. In a separate bowl, mix together cottage cheese, egg, and black pepper.

4. Spoon about ⅓ of the spaghetti sauce mixture over bottom of crock.

5. Cover that with 4 uncooked lasagna noodles, breaking to make them fit.

6. Spread with half the cottage cheese–egg mixture.

7. Sprinkle with ⅓ of the mozzarella.

8. Spoon over half the remaining spaghetti sauce mixture.

9. Cover with remaining 4 lasagna noodles.

10. Spread with remaining cottage cheese–egg mix.

11. Sprinkle with half the remaining mozzarella.

12. Spoon over last of spaghetti sauce mixture.

13. Scatter with last of mozzarella cheese.

14. Spread evenly with grated Parmesan cheese.

15. Cover. Put in fridge for 8 hours or overnight.

16. When ready to cook, cover. Set on Low for 4–4½ hours, or until lasagna is hot in the center and noodles are fully cooked.

17. Let stand 15 minutes before serving to allow lasagna to firm up.

INSTANT POT

Macaroni and Cheese

Hope Comerford, Clinton Township, MI

Makes 8 servings
Prep. Time: 5 minutes & Cooking Time: 4 minutes

1 lb. uncooked elbow macaroni

2 cups water

2 cups chicken or vegetable broth

4 Tbsp. butter

1 tsp. salt

½ tsp. pepper

1 tsp. hot sauce

1 tsp. mustard powder

½–1 cup heavy cream or milk

1½ cups shredded sharp cheddar cheese

1½ cups shredded Monterey Jack cheese

1. Place the macaroni, water, broth, butter, salt, pepper, hot sauce, and mustard powder into the inner pot of the Instant Pot.

2. Secure the lid and set the vent to sealing. Manually set the cook time for 4 minutes.

3. When the cook time is over, manually release the pressure.

4. When the pin drops, remove the lid and stir in the cream, starting with ½ cup. Begin stirring in the shredded cheese, 1 cup at a time. If the sauce ends up being too thin, let it sit a while and it will thicken up.

Variation:

If you want the mac and cheese to have a crust on top, pour the mac and cheese from the Instant Pot into an oven-safe baking dish. Top with additional cheese and bake in a 325°F oven for about 15 minutes.

Serving suggestion:

This would be great served alongside Potluck Baked Corn on page 189 and Southwestern Cauliflower on page 190.

Macaroni and Cheese

Martha Hershey, Ronks, PA
Marcia S. Myer, Manheim, PA
LeAnne Nolt, Leola, PA
Ellen Ranck, Gap, PA
Mary Sommerfeld, Lancaster, PA
Kathryn Yoder, Minot, ND
Janie Steele, Moore, OK

Makes 6 servings
Prep. Time: 30 minutes ⚬ *Cooking Time: 3–4 hours* ⚬ *Ideal slow-cooker size: 4-qt.*

8-oz. pkg. dry macaroni, cooked

2 Tbsp. oil

13-oz. can evaporated milk (fat-free will work)

1½ cups milk

1 tsp. salt

3 cups (about ½ lb.) shredded cheese: cheddar, or American, or Velveeta, or a combination

2–4 Tbsp. melted butter

2 Tbsp. finely chopped onion

1. In slow cooker, toss cooked macaroni in oil. Stir in remaining ingredients.

2. Cover. Cook on Low 3–4 hours.

Serving suggestions:

If you wish, mix ½ cup breadcrumbs and 2 Tbsp. melted butter together. Sprinkle over dish just before serving. Or top instead with crushed potato chips. Serve alongside Very Special Spinach on page 194.

Variations:

1. Use 3 cups evaporated milk, instead of 13-oz. can evaporated milk and 1½ cups milk.

2. Add more onion, up to ¼ cup total, in Step 1.

3. Add ½ tsp. pepper in Step 1.

4. Add 4 sliced hotdogs the last hour of cooking.

Black Bean Burritos

Esther Nafziger, La Junta, CO

Makes 6–8 servings

Prep. Time: 20 minutes ⚜ *Cooking Time: 7–12 hours* ⚜ *Ideal slow-cooker size: 5-qt.*

2 cups dried black beans

7 cups water

Hot chilies, diced, to taste

½ cup chopped onion

⅓ cup salsa, as hot or mild as you like

3 cloves garlic, minced

1 tsp. dried oregano

1 tsp. chili powder

2 tsp. salt

½ tsp. black pepper

6–8 flour tortillas

Chopped lettuce

Fresh tomatoes, chopped, or salsa

1½ cups shredded cheese of your choice

Serving suggestion:

This would be great served alongside Potluck Baked Corn on page 189 and Southwestern Cauliflower on page 190.

1. Grease interior of slow-cooker crock.

2. Sort and rinse dried beans.

3. Place in crock. Add water.

4. Cover. Cook on Low 9–10 hours, or on High 6–7 hours, or until beans are as tender as you like them.

5. Drain off any cooking liquid.

6. Stir hot chilies, onion, salsa, garlic, oregano, chili powder, salt, and pepper into cooked beans in crock.

7. Cover. Cook on High 1 hour, or on Low 2 hours, or until veggies are as tender as you want.

8. Spoon filling down center of each tortilla. Top with lettuce, tomatoes or salsa, and cheese.

9. Fold top and bottom of each tortilla over filling. Roll up to serve.

Tip:

Leftover filling freezes well.

Cornbread-Topped Frijoles

Andy Wagner, Quarryville, PA

Makes 8–10 servings

Prep. Time: 20–30 minutes ❧ *Cooking Time: 3 hours* ❧ *Ideal slow-cooker size: 5-qt.*

1 medium onion, chopped

1 medium green bell pepper, chopped

2 cloves garlic, minced

16-oz. can kidney beans, rinsed and drained

15-oz. can pinto beans, rinsed and drained

14½-oz. can diced tomatoes, undrained

8-oz. can tomato sauce

1 tsp. chili powder

½ tsp. coarsely ground black pepper

¼ tsp. hot pepper sauce

Cornbread Topping:

½ cup flour

½ cup yellow cornmeal

2 tsp. sugar

1 tsp. baking powder

¼ tsp. salt

1 egg, lightly beaten

¾ cup skim milk

½ cup cream-style corn

1½ Tbsp. canola oil

1. Grease interior of slow-cooker crock.

2. Stir onion, green pepper, garlic, both beans, tomatoes, tomato sauce, chili powder, black pepper, and hot sauce together in crock.

3. Cover. Cook on High 1 hour.

4. While frijoles are cooking, in a large bowl, mix the flour, cornmeal, sugar, baking powder, and salt.

5. In another bowl, combine egg, milk, corn, and oil.

6. Add wet ingredients to dry, mixing well.

7. Spoon evenly over frijoles in crock. Do not stir.

8. Cover. Cook on High 2 more hours, or until a toothpick inserted in center of cornbread comes out clean.

Serving suggestion:

This would be great served alongside Very Special Spinach on page 194.

Tuna Salad Casserole

Charlotte Fry, Saint Charles, MO
Esther Becker Gordonville, PA

Makes 4 servings
Prep. Time: 10 minutes ⚬ *Cooking Time: 5–8 hours* ⚬ *Ideal slow-cooker size: 4-qt.*

2 (7-oz.) cans tuna

10¾-oz. can cream of celery soup

3 hard-boiled eggs, chopped

½–1½ cups diced celery

½ cup diced onion

½ cup mayonnaise

¼ tsp. ground pepper

1½ cups crushed potato chips, *divided*

1. Combine all ingredients except ¼ cup potato chips in slow cooker. Top with remaining chips.

2. Cover. Cook on Low 5–8 hours.

Serving suggestion:

This would be great served alongside Slow-Cooker Scalloped Potatoes on page 184.

Side Dishes

Perfect White Rice

Hope Comerford, Clinton Township, MI

Makes 4 servings
Prep. Time: 2 minutes *Cooking Time: 8 minutes*

1 cup uncooked white rice

1 tsp. olive oil, or coconut oil

1 cup water

Pinch salt

1. Rinse rice under cold running water until the water runs clear, then pour into the inner pot.

2. Add oil, water, and salt to the inner pot.

3. Lock the lid and set the steam valve to its sealing position. Select the Rice button and set to cook for 8 minutes.

4. Allow the pressure to release naturally for 10 minutes and then release any remaining pressure manually.

5. Fluff the rice with a fork and serve.

Wild Rice

Ruth S. Weaver, Reinholds, PA

Makes 4–5 servings
Prep. Time: 10 minutes ⚶ Cooking Time: 2½–3 hours ⚶ Ideal slow-cooker size: 3-qt.

I cup wild rice, or wild rice mixture,
uncooked

½ cup sliced mushrooms

½ cup diced onion

½ cup diced green, or red, peppers

I Tbsp. oil

½ tsp. salt

¼ tsp. pepper

2½ cups chicken broth

1. Layer rice and vegetables in slow cooker. Pour oil, salt, and pepper over vegetables. Stir.

2. Heat chicken broth. Pour over ingredients in slow cooker.

3. Cover. Cook on High 2½–3 hours, or until rice is soft and liquid is absorbed.

Cheesy Broccoli Rice Casserole

Hope Comerford, Clinton Township, MI

Makes 4 servings

Prep. Time: 10 minutes · Cooking Time: 6 minutes

1 Tbsp. olive oil

¾ cup chopped onion

4-oz. fresh sliced mushrooms

2 cups rice

1 tsp. garlic powder

1 tsp. salt

¼ tsp. pepper

2½ cups chicken broth, *divided*

2 cups chopped broccoli florets

1½ cups shredded cheddar cheese

1. Set the Instant Pot to Sauté mode and heat the oil.

2. Sauté the onion and mushrooms in the oil for about 3 minutes. Press Cancel.

3. Add the rice, garlic powder, salt, pepper, and 2 cups of the broth. Stir.

4. Secure the lid and set the vent to sealing. Manually set the cook time for 5 minutes on high pressure.

5. When the cook time is over, manually release the pressure. When the pin drops, remove the lid.

6. Stir in the broccoli and remaining ½ cup of broth.

7. Secure the lid and set the vent to sealing. Manually set the cook time for 1 minute on high pressure.

8. When the cook time is over, manually release the pressure.

9. When the pin drops, remove the lid and stir in the cheese.

Perfect Pinto Beans

Hope Comerford, Clinton Township, MI

Makes 8 servings
Prep. Time: 2 minutes   Cooking Time: 50 minutes

1 large onion, chopped

1 lb. dry pinto beans, sorted and rinsed

6 cups vegetable or chicken broth

2 bay leaves

1½ tsp. sea salt

1 tsp. cumin

½ tsp. paprika

¼ tsp. pepper

1. Place all ingredients into the inner pot of the Instant Pot.

2. Secure the lid and set the vent to sealing. Manually set the cook time for 50 minutes on high pressure.

3. When the cook time is over, let the pressure release naturally for 15 minutes, then manually release the remaining pressure. Remove the bay leaves before serving.

Garlicky Black Beans

INSTANT POT

Hope Comerford, Clinton Township, MI

Makes 10 servings
Prep. Time: 10 minutes 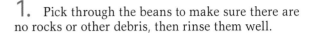 *Cooking Time: 25 minutes*

1 lb. dry black beans

1 cup chopped onion

3 cloves garlic

2 tsp. sea salt

¼ tsp. pepper

4 cups vegetable broth

2 cups water

1. Pick through the beans to make sure there are no rocks or other debris, then rinse them well.

2. Place the beans, onion, garlic, sea salt, and pepper into the inner pot of the Instant Pot.

3. Pour the broth and water over the top.

4. Secure the lid and set the vent to sealing. Manually set the cook time for 25 minutes on high pressure.

5. When cook time is up, let the pressure release naturally.

Slow-Cooker Scalloped Potatoes

Ruth S. Weaver, Reinholds, PA

Makes 10 servings

Prep. Time: 20 minutes ❧ Cooking Time: 4–10 hours ❧ Ideal slow-cooker size: 4-qt.

½ tsp. cream of tartar

1 cup water

8–10 medium potatoes, thinly sliced

Half an onion, chopped

Salt and pepper to taste

1 cup grated American, or cheddar, cheese

10¾-oz. can cream of celery, or mushroom, or chicken, soup

1 tsp. paprika

1. Dissolve cream of tartar in water. Add potatoes and toss together. Drain.

2. Place half of potatoes in slow cooker. Sprinkle with onion, salt, pepper, and half of cheese.

3. Repeat with remaining potatoes and cheese.

4. Spoon soup over the top. Sprinkle with paprika.

5. Cover. Cook on Low 8–10 hours, or on High 4 hours.

Variations:

1. For thicker scalloped potatoes, sprinkle each layer of potatoes with 2 Tbsp. flour.

    —Ruth Hershey, Paradise, PA

2. Instead of sprinkling the layers of potatoes with grated cheese, place ¼ lb. Velveeta, or American, cheese slices over top during last 30 minutes of cooking.

    —Pat Bishop, Bedminster, PA; Mary Ellen Musser, Reinholds, PA; and Annabelle Unternahrer, Shipshewana, IN

SLOW COOKER

Cabbage and Potatoes

Deb Kepiro, Strasburg, PA

Makes 4 servings
Prep. Time: 15 minutes ⚘ *Cooking Time: 3–6 hours* ⚘ *Ideal slow-cooker size: 4-qt.*

1 small head green cabbage, sliced thinly

14 small red-skinned potatoes, cut in 1-inch chunks

1 small onion, diced

3 Tbsp. olive oil

2 Tbsp. balsamic vinegar

1 tsp. kosher salt

½ tsp. black pepper

1. Put all ingredients in slow cooker. Mix well.

2. Cover and cook on High for 3 hours or on Low 6 hours, until potatoes are as tender as you like them.

Vegetable Medley

Janie Steele, Moore, OK

Makes 6–8 servings

Prep. Time: 25–30 minutes 🌢 Cooking Time: 1½–2 hours 🌢 Ideal slow-cooker size: 4-qt.

Large raw potato, peeled and cut into small cubes

2 onions, chopped

2 carrots, sliced thin

¾ cup uncooked long-grain rice

2 Tbsp. lemon juice

⅓ cup plus 2 Tbsp. olive oil

2 (1-lb.) cans diced tomatoes, *divided*

1 cup water, *divided*

Large green pepper, chopped

2 zucchini squash, chopped

2 Tbsp. parsley, chopped

Half a 1-lb. pkg. frozen green peas

1 Tbsp. salt

1 cup grated cheese

Hot sauce, *optional*

1. Combine potato, onions, carrots, rice, lemon juice, olive oil, 1 can of tomatoes, and ½ cup water in slow cooker.

2. Cover and cook on High, 1 hour.

3. Stir in remaining ingredients, except grated cheese and hot sauce. Cover and cook 30–60 minutes, or until vegetables are tender but not mushy.

4. Serve in bowls, topped with grated cheese. Pass hot sauce to be added individually.

Potluck Baked Corn

Velma Stauffer, Akron, PA

Makes 10–12 servings

Prep. Time: 15 minutes   Cooking Time: 3–4 hours   Ideal slow-cooker size: 6-qt.

2 qts. frozen corn, thawed and drained

4 eggs, beaten

2 tsp. salt

1¾ cups 2% or whole milk

2 Tbsp. melted butter

3 Tbsp. sugar

6 Tbsp. flour

1. Mix all ingredients in mixing bowl until well combined.

2. Pour into greased slow cooker.

3. Cover and cook on High 3–4 hours until set in the middle and lightly browned at edges.

Southwestern Cauliflower

Hope Comerford, Clinton Township, MI

Makes 6–8 servings
Prep. Time: 5 minutes ⚬ Cooking Time: 1 minute

1 cup water

1 large head cauliflower, cut into florets

1 Tbsp. olive oil

½ tsp. smoked paprika

½ tsp. chili powder

½ tsp. cumin

½ tsp. sea salt

¼ tsp. oregano

⅛ tsp. black pepper

1. Pour the water into the inner pot of the Instant Pot, then place the steamer basket on top.

2. Put the cauliflower florets into a medium-sized bowl and pour over the olive oil and sprinkle the seasonings over the top. Toss to coat everything well. Pour into the steamer basket.

3. Secure the lid and set the vent to sealing. Manually set the cook time for 1 minute on high pressure.

4. When cook time is up, manually release the pressure.

5. When the pin drops, carefully remove the lid and serve the cauliflower.

Orange Glazed Carrots

Cyndie Marrara, Port Matilda, PA

Makes 6 servings

Prep. Time: 5–10 minutes   ⚬   Cooking Time: 3–4 hours   ⚬   Ideal slow-cooker size: 3½-qt.

32-oz. (2 lb.) pkg. baby carrots
½ cup packed brown sugar
½ cup orange juice
3 Tbsp. butter, or margarine
¾ tsp. cinnamon
¼ tsp. nutmeg
2 Tbsp. cornstarch
¼ cup water

1. Combine all ingredients except cornstarch and water in slow cooker.

2. Cover. Cook on Low 3–4 hours, until carrots are tender crisp.

3. Put carrots in serving dish and keep warm, reserving cooking juices. Put reserved juices in small saucepan. Bring to boil.

4. Mix cornstarch and water in small bowl until blended. Add to juices. Boil one minute or until thickened, stirring constantly.

5. Pour over carrots and serve.

Broccoli with Garlic

Andrea Cunningham, Arlington, KS

Makes 4 servings
Prep. Time: 5 minutes ⚘ *Cooking Time: as long as it takes to come to pressure*

½ cup cold water

I head (about 5 cups) broccoli, cut into long pieces all the way through (you will eat the stems)

I Tbsp. olive oil

2–3 cloves garlic, sliced thin

⅛ tsp. pepper

1. Place a steamer basket into the inner pot along with the cold water. Put the broccoli into the steamer basket.

2. Secure the lid and set the vent to sealing.

3. Manually set the cook time for 0 minutes on high pressure.

4. Manually release the pressure when it's done. Press Cancel.

5. When the pin drops, open the lid and place the broccoli into an ice bath or run under cold water to stop it from cooking. Let it air dry.

6. Carefully remove the water from the inner pot and wipe it dry.

7. Set the Instant Pot to the Sauté function and heat the oil.

8. Sauté the garlic for 1 minute, then add the broccoli, sprinkle it with the pepper, and continue to sauté for an additional 1 to 2 minutes.

9. Just before serving, squeeze lemon juice over the top.

Very Special Spinach

Jeanette Oberholtzer, Manheim, PA

Makes 8 servings
Prep. Time: 10 minutes   Cooking Time: 5 hours   Ideal slow-cooker size: 4-qt.

3 (10-oz.) boxes frozen spinach, thawed and drained

2 cups cottage cheese

1½ cups grated cheddar cheese

3 eggs

¼ cup flour

1 tsp. salt

½ cup melted butter, or margarine

1. Mix together all ingredients.

2. Pour into slow cooker.

3. Cook on High 1 hour. Reduce heat to Low and cook 4 more hours.

Green Beans Caesar

Carol Shirk, Leola, PA

Makes 6–8 servings

Prep. Time: 15 minutes   ⚜   Cooking Time: 2½–3½ hours   ⚜   Ideal slow-cooker size: 3–4-qt.

1 ½ lb. green beans, ends trimmed

2 Tbsp. olive oil

1 Tbsp. red wine vinegar

1 Tbsp. minced garlic

Salt and pepper to taste

½ tsp. dried basil

½ tsp. dried oregano

¼ cup plain breadcrumbs

¼ cup grated Parmesan cheese

1 Tbsp. butter, melted

1. In slow cooker, combine green beans, olive oil, vinegar, garlic, salt and pepper, basil, and oregano.

2. Cover and cook on High for 2–3 hours, until green beans are as soft as you like them. Stir.

3. Combine breadcrumbs, Parmesan, and butter. Sprinkle over green beans and cook an additional 30 minutes on High with lid off.

Metric Equivalent Measurements

If you're accustomed to using metric measurements, I don't want you to be inconvenienced by the imperial measurements I use in this book.

Use this handy chart, too, to figure out the size of the slow cooker you'll need for each recipe.

Weight (Dry Ingredients)

1 oz		30 g
4 oz	¼ lb	120 g
8 oz	½ lb	240 g
12 oz	¾ lb	360 g
16 oz	1 lb	480 g
32 oz	2 lb	960 g

Slow-Cooker Sizes

1-quart	0.96 l
2-quart	1.92 l
3-quart	2.88 l
4-quart	3.84 l
5-quart	4.80 l
6-quart	5.76 l
7-quart	6.72 l
8-quart	7.68 l

Volume (Liquid Ingredients)

½ tsp.		2 ml
1 tsp.		5 ml
1 Tbsp.	½ fl oz	15 ml
2 Tbsp.	1 fl oz	30 ml
¼ cup	2 fl oz	60 ml
⅓ cup	3 fl oz	80 ml
½ cup	4 fl oz	120 ml
⅔ cup	5 fl oz	160 ml
¾ cup	6 fl oz	180 ml
1 cup	8 fl oz	240 ml
1 pt	16 fl oz	480 ml
1 qt	32 fl oz	960 ml

Length

¼ in	6 mm
½ in	13 mm
¾ in	19 mm
1 in	25 mm
6 in	15 cm
12 in	30 cm

Recipe & Ingredient Index

About the Author

Hope Comerford is a mom, wife, elementary music teacher, blogger, recipe developer, public speaker, Young Living Essential Oils essential oil enthusiast/educator, and published author. In 2013, she was diagnosed with a severe gluten intolerance and since then has spent many hours creating easy, practical, and delicious gluten-free recipes that can be enjoyed by both those who are affected by gluten and those who are not.

Growing up, Hope spent many hours in the kitchen with her Meme (grandmother) and her love for cooking grew from there. While working on her master's degree when her daughter was young, Hope turned to her slow cookers for some salvation and sanity. It was from there she began truly experimenting with recipes and quickly learned she had the ability to get a little more creative in the kitchen and develop her own recipes.

In 2010, Hope started her blog, *A Busy Mom's Slow Cooker Adventures*, to simply share the recipes she was making with her family and friends. She never imagined people all over the world would begin visiting her page and sharing her recipes with others as well. In 2013, Hope self-published her first cookbook, *Slow Cooker Recipes 10 Ingredients or Less and Gluten-Free*, and then later wrote *The Gluten-Free Slow Cooker*.

Hope became the new brand ambassador and author of Fix-It and Forget-It in mid-2016. Since then, she has brought her excitement and creativeness to the Fix-It and Forget-It brand. Through Fix-It and Forget-It, she has written *Fix-It and Forget-It Healthy One-Pot Meals Cookbook*, *Fix-It and Forget-It Slow Cooker Freezer Meals Cookbook*, *Fix-It and Forget-It Freezer to Instant Pot Cookbook*, *Welcome Home 30-Minute Meals*, *Fix-It and Forget-It Everyday Instant Pot Favorites*, and many more.

Hope lives in the city of Clinton Township, Michigan, near Metro Detroit. She has been happily married to her husband and best friend, Justin, since 2008. Together they have two children, Ella and Gavin, who are her motivation, inspiration, and heart. In her spare time, Hope enjoys traveling, singing, cooking, reading books, working on wooden puzzles, spending time with friends and family, and relaxing.